Skills for New Managers

Other titles in the Briefcase Books series include:

To learn more about titles in the Briefcase Books series go to
www.briefcasebooks.com
You'll find the tables of contents, downloadable sample chapters, information on the authors, discussion guides for using these books in training programs, and more.

A
Briefcase
Book

Skills for New Managers

Morey Stettner

McGraw-Hill

New York San Francisco Washington, D.C. Auckland Bogotá
Caracas Lisbon London Madrid Mexico City Milan
Montreal New Delhi San Juan Singapore
Sydney Tokyo Toronto

The McGraw·Hill Companies

11 12 13 14 15 16 17 18 AGM/AGM 0 9 8 7 6 5 4 3

ISBN 0-07-135618-5

Library of Congress Cataloging-in-Publication Data

Stettner, Morey
   Skills for new managers / Morey Stettner
      p. cm. -- Briefcase Book
   ISBN 0-07-135618-5
      1. Leadership. 2. Employee motivation. 3. Management.
      I. Title. II. Series
   HD57.7.S736 2000
   658.4-dc21
                                                      99-462320

This is a CWL Publishing Enterprises Book, developed and produced for McGraw-Hill by CWL Publishing Enterprises, John A. Woods, President. For more information, contact CWL Publishing Enterprises, 3010 Irvington Way, Madison, WI 53713-3414, www.cwlpub.com. Robert Magnan served as editor. For McGraw-Hill, the sponsoring editor was Catherine Dassopoulos, the publisher was Jeffrey Krames, the editing supervisor was John M. Morriss, and the production supervisor was Elizabeth Strange.

Printed and bound by Quebecor World/Martinsburg

McGraw-Hill books are available at special quantity discounts to use as pre-miums and sales promotions, or for use in corporate training programs. For more information, please write to the Director of Special Sales, McGraw-Hill, 2 Penn Plaza, New York, NY 10121. Or contact your local bookstore.

This book is printed on recycled, acid-free paper containing a mini-mum of 50% recycled de-inked fiber.

Contents

Preface

There's an old joke that generations of disgruntled employees like to tell each other.

"You know what the definition of manager is, don't you?"

"No, tell me."

"A manager is the person who sees the visitors so that everyone else can get the work done."

Maybe that's funny to some people. But now that you're a manager, it's your job to laugh *with* your staff, rather than having them laugh *at* you.

There are thousands of managers out there, all trying to recruit, train, and motivate their staffs. They all want the same thing: to please their bosses, to earn the respect of their employees, and, above all, to avoid the headaches that so often come with people management.

As a new manager, you may find the whole task daunting. In your old job, you could excel by mastering a specialty. You showed up every day, carved out an area of expertise, and thrived by performing at a level that impressed higher-ups at your organization.

Now you've earned a reward: a staff to manage. From now on, your success no longer depends on just your technical abilities and specialized knowledge. You will prosper only if other people do their jobs well. And if they fail, you'll pay the price.

The best managers embrace the challenge with gusto. They build trust with each employee one day at a time, learning how to woo even the most difficult types of workers to push harder, think differently, and stage experiments that help them produce better results. They set high standards and "walk the talk."

When problems arise, they mediate them with poise and fairness. During organizational upheavals and wrenching change, they keep employees informed and provide a rock of stability. When setbacks strike, they do not mope and whine about forces they cannot control; instead, they reassure their staffs and redirect everyone's focus on what matters most.

Why Read This Book?

Do you have a mentor who helps you unlock all the secrets of managing? If you do, great. This book will serve as an added resource, a way to cross-check whether the advice you're getting squares with some of the latest views on enlightened management.

If you lack a mentor, then consider this book a friendly substitute. While we can't take your calls when you're confronting an emergency or provide a shoulder to cry on when you're going bonkers at work, we can give you plenty of practical pointers on how to handle a range of situations that you'll no doubt face as a manager.

We won't kid you: effective management requires more than reading this book and nodding with approval when you come across a tip or technique that appeals to you. *You must apply what you read.* By sampling the tools you're about to learn, you can evaluate to what extent they work for you and modify them as needed. People are not mathematical equations, so managing them is a fuzzier and more free-form process than inputting hard data. But as long as you commit to putting into practice what we're about to discuss, we promise your time spent reading this book will pay off.

Overview of the Book

In the first chapter, you'll develop a model of the successful manager. This becomes your template for what follows. Once you know what kind of traits, skills, and behaviors will make you manage more effectively, you can mold yourself to excel.

Chapter 2 pierces some of the most prevalent myths of people management. If you're guided by mistaken notions of what it takes to lead employees, then your faulty assumptions can interfere with your better judgment and sabotage your ability to manage.

The purpose of Chapter 3 is to help you hit the ground running. Your first month as a new manager will be traumatic enough without having to confront needless crises. By establishing momentum and taking preventive steps to stamp out problems before they arise, you can gain confidence and impress others with your take-charge leadership.

Chapters 4 and 5 work together to give you pointers to polish your communication skills. We begin with the all-important art of listening, a vastly overlooked skill that every strong manager must possess. You may bring great technical ability and plenty of enthusiasm to your new job, but if you hog the spotlight and interrupt constantly, you doom yourself to mediocrity.

In Chapter 5, we move from listening to talking. You'll need to say what's on your mind to employees and to your managers. You'll also need to be able to ask intelligent questions and organize your thoughts in a tight, appealing package. Persuasion flows from preparation. When you think before you speak, you can win over almost anyone and turn adversaries into allies.

Chapter 6 examines the mysteries of motivation. Many new managers stumble in their efforts to rally the troops. They assume rah-rah theatrics work best, when in fact the best way to motivate is to observe others and identify what matters most to them.

Chapters 7 and 8 guide you through two of the toughest aspects of management: giving criticism and doling out discipline. You probably dread both of these tasks. But if you learn to do them well, you can proceed with the knowledge that you're a fair-minded, respected manager.

The key to criticizing employees is helping them realize for themselves how their performance can improve. By steering clear of harsh generalizations and instead describing a specific activity in neutral terms, you remove personality from the equation and increase the odds your criticism will pay off.

When you have to discipline an employee, you need to understand when and how to do this. Discipline, after all, is about helping people who, either by intention or misunderstanding of the rules, disrupt the operations of your group. When you do this well, you bring people back into line and help make them better employees.

Chapter 9 gives you the tools to organize yourself. Many new managers trip themselves up by losing track of time and getting buried in minutiae. By tracking your work and avoiding time-killing tasks, you can boost your productivity and squeeze the most out of every hour.

Every manager must delegate, and that's the subject of Chapter 10. It's easy to bark orders and await results. But your style of giving directions will largely determine whether your employees comply or rebel.

Chapter 11 focuses on managing your manager rather than your workers. Keeping higher-ups apprised of your progress and maintaining open lines of communication can eliminate misunderstandings and ensure that you get the credit you deserve for your efforts.

Finally, in Chapter 12, you'll learn how to capitalize on your new role as manager to climb the ladder. That involves networking. The wider your web of contacts both inside and outside your organization, the faster you can nab promotions or pounce on career opportunities.

Special Features

The idea behind the books in the Briefcase Series is to give you practical information written in a friendly person-to-person style. The chapters are short, deal with tactical issues, and include lots of examples. They also feature numerous boxes designed to give you different types of specific information. Here's a description of the boxes you'll find in this book.

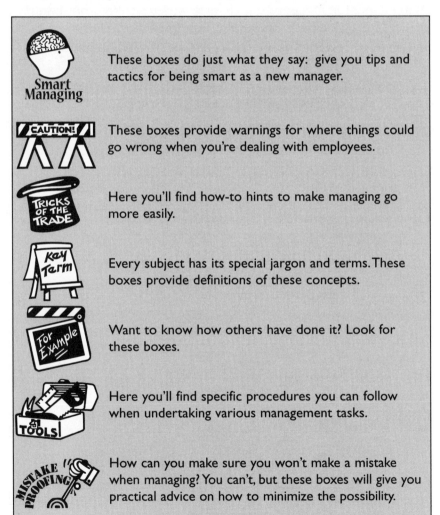

These boxes do just what they say: give you tips and tactics for being smart as a new manager.

These boxes provide warnings for where things could go wrong when you're dealing with employees.

Here you'll find how-to hints to make managing go more easily.

Every subject has its special jargon and terms. These boxes provide definitions of these concepts.

Want to know how others have done it? Look for these boxes.

Here you'll find specific procedures you can follow when undertaking various management tasks.

How can you make sure you won't make a mistake when managing? You can't, but these boxes will give you practical advice on how to minimize the possibility.

About the Author

Morey Stettner is a writer and communication-skills consultant in Portsmouth, NH. He's the author of *The Art of Winning Conversation* (Prentice Hall), which shows you how to listen and win over others in your personal and professional life. He is editor of *Working Smart* and *Executive Strategies*, two monthly newsletters published by the National Institute of Business Management in McLean, VA. He also writes weekly front-page articles on effective management for *Investor's Business Daily*. A dynamic speaker and seminar leader, he has led hundreds of training programs across the United States on topics such as sales skills, public speaking, and attentive listening. You can e-mail him at may12@concentric.net.

The *Successful* New Manager

R andy's dream has come true. An insurance underwriter for the last four years, he can finally call himself a manager. His boss recently told him, "You've worked hard, the agents like you, and your results have been outstanding. So we're going to put you in charge of one of our underwriting units. Our hope is you'll teach your employees how you do it, and your success will rub off on them."

Just like that, 10 employees now report to Randy. He walks into his new office (a real office, not a cubicle!) and looks around in a daze. He has wanted to manage a staff ever since he visited his division head's huge home many years ago and noticed how well a "boss" could live. And he figures that once he proves that he can handle a group of crusty, cynical underwriters and help them boost their results, the sky's the limit for him.

Who's Your Model?

Like so many new managers, Randy assumes that he can do the job better than others who've come before him because he realizes what mistakes not to make. He's had seven bosses in his career, and he knows exactly what they did right and wrong. The same thing happens when proud parents hold their newborn and declare confidently to each other, "Let's raise this adorable baby the right way, not like our parents did it!"

You may think you know what it takes to manage well. After all, you're an earnest straight-shooter who gets along well with a wide range of people. You like challenges and you dread boring routines. Experienced managers have told you that "every day is different" when you're in charge of a staff, and that sounds just fine with you.

But the real test of your management skills rests on your ability to grow into the job. No newly minted manager can possibly anticipate what it's like to direct people. Each day brings weird scenarios you could never predict, from the clerk who bursts into tears for no apparent reason (what do you do?) to the disgruntled veteran who issues a veiled threat against you and your company (now what?). As perhaps you can tell, managing is more than setting goals and organizing people to accomplish them. Lots of things need to be taken care of between setting goals and accomplishing them.

There's no way this or any book can show you how to respond to every type of human problem you may encounter. But a book can help you sharpen your natural leadership skills and learn how to model yourself after effective managers so that you analyze how they would handle a similar situation.

By imagining how a top-notch manager would manage various scenarios, you give yourself a road map to follow.

My Favorite Manager

Smart Managing Think of the best boss you ever had. If no one pops to mind, consider a strong leader you know, such as a sports coach or a volunteer coordinator at your community center. Complete these sentences:

1. When faced with adversity, this manager will _____.
2. To improve teamwork, this manager will _____.
3. When explaining a concept, this manager will _____.
4. To keep control of an unruly group, this manager will _____.
5. Employees respect this manager because _____.

This little exercise will help you focus on appropriate and effective behaviors and tactics for dealing with people.

The individual you admire most serves as your template. Even if you're not sure how this person would deal with specific issues or perform certain tasks, trying to picture such behaviors can help.

In deciding whom to model, consider your corporate culture. Say you work in a laid-back environment filled with brainy graduate students engaged in medical testing or software programming. In such a setting, you want to promote a calm, cerebral, and creative atmosphere where your employees can operate at their best. Trying to model yourself after a loud, hard-charging executive whom you admire will backfire, because those kinds of rah-rah theatrics will fall flat in such an intellectually driven office.

Also think about how you might choose the person whom you seek to emulate. You don't want to select a role model just because she's your best friend or you share certain interests. It's best to model yourself after a manager whom you respect more than like (though the two are certainly not mutually exclusive). You want to learn from someone who takes action decisively and exemplifies the kind of behaviors that you think would make you an effective manager.

Rating Your Leadership

The more you know yourself, the better you'll manage. If you lack a strong sense of who you are and what you believe, you'll get manipulated by more forceful personalities who can tell you're a pushover. They'll feed you what you like to hear. And they'll press your hot buttons when they want to rile you.

You need to develop a strong spine to manage. If it hasn't happened yet, the day will come when you'll need to state an unpopular position and stick to it, despite disappointment from employees and even derision from bosses. You'll need to believe in yourself when doubts swirl around you, especially as the stakes mount and the pressure builds. That's when your reserves of poise and confidence will sustain you.

To gain self-awareness, take the following diagnostic tests. Your ratings will help you uncover the strengths and weaknesses that influence how you manage.

Test 1: Patience

Rate yourself using this 1-to-5 scale:

1. Never
2. Occasionally
3. Sometimes
4. Usually
5. Always

Total 12

When I tell someone to do something and they don't do it, I say it again in a firmer tone. _3_
When someone talks too slowly, I interrupt. _3_
When I see someone do something wrong, I instantly point it out. _2_
When someone keeps me waiting more than a minute or two, I resent it. _2_
When someone doesn't answer my question right away, I cut in and repeat it. _2_

Add up your score. If it's 17 or more, you could stand to lighten up and calm down. You need to relax a little. Your impatience might reflect an overly controlling mind-set. If you scored 16 or less, note any 4s or 5s. These indicate areas you can work on that will lower your blood pressure and raise your ability to build trust and gain compliance.

Test 2: Communication Skills

Rate yourself using the 1-to-5 scale above:

Total 14

When I ask a question, I'm very curious to hear the answer. _5_
I like to speak in front of groups. _1_
If I disagree, I confirm I've understood the other person before I give my view. _4_
If I need to cover many points, I outline what I want to say ahead of time. _2_
When I give instructions or explain complex ideas, I number each item. _2_

If you scored 15 or less, you're probably losing opportunities to bond with others. Your employees can tell if you're distracted or uninterested in what they have to say, and they won't like it. And if you ramble or hop from topic to topic aimlessly, they're liable to tune out or lose track of your point. Disliking public speaking won't necessarily kill your chances of managing well, but by developing at least some skills you can add a valuable weapon to your management arsenal.

Test 3: Ethics   Total 21

Rate yourself on using the 1-to-5 scale on the preceding page:

I set an example of the high ethical standard I want my staff to follow. _4_

If I'm in an ethical bind, I'll talk about the situation with a wise mentor. _5_

I prefer to admit doing something wrong than to cover it up and hope I don't get caught. _4_

I apply "the sniff test" when confronting an ethical dilemma: if it smells bad, I don't do it. _3_

I'm at peace with my ethical behavior. _5_

A score of 18 or below should alert you to some questionable attitudes about right and wrong. If your total falls under 15, then you might as well kiss your management career goodbye now rather than wait for the inevitable downfall later.

There are other aspects that are important to a strong sense of yourself and your leadership ability in addition to patience, communication skills, and ethics. But those three are basic and vital. Now, you may be thinking, 'Patience and communication skills, of course, because a manager must work well with people in order to get the job done. But ethics? In business?'

Yes, ethics! We all make moral decisions everyday, whether we realize it or not. If we break rules routinely or grab whatever we can take without a moment's hesitation, then we doom ourselves to alienating the very employees we need to win over— and we set a very poor example. Expedience has its place, but crossing ethical boundaries whenever the situation warrants it undermines your credibility as a leader. Sure, you can probably get away with managing by deception, double-crossing, and denial, but only if you're willing to lose everything in a flash—or to gradually corrupt your employees and lose it all slowly and painfully. As in all of life's activities, integrity is an important characteristic of any manager.

Drafting Your Own "Management Credo"

Earlier in this chapter, you thought about the best boss you ever had. Now it's time to consider the kind of boss you want to be.

Developing a credo—or set of beliefs—can serve as a constant reminder of what you want to achieve in your new job and how. This process means more than hashing out detailed, work-related objectives such as setting projected annual revenues for your unit or maintaining low turnover. It's loftier than that. You should prepare for the challenges of management by identifying the traits you want to embody and the commitments you're willing to make to yourself to succeed.

To begin, set aside 30 minutes during a calm, unhurried part of the day, perhaps Sunday morning when you're not distracted by workaday pressures. Plant yourself in front of your computer—or settle down with pen and paper—and pretend it's a year from now.

Ask yourself, "How do I want to be perceived as a boss by an employee who has been reporting to me for the past year?"

Answer this question *from the employee's perspective*. Play the role of one of your direct reports and imagine giving yourself a performance review. Address key areas such as communication skills, leadership, reliability, motivational style, and fostering teamwork.

TRICKS OF THE TRADE

What's Your Grade?
Think back to when you were an employee, probably not so long ago. Now imagine that you have the opportunity as employee to do a performance review of yourself as a boss. What categories would you use? How would you rate yourself from 1 to 10 or grade yourself from A to F? Be realistic, fair, and objective!

If you've treated this exercise seriously, you should come away with a revealing self-assessment of your managerial strengths and shortcomings. Armed with this information, you're now ready to compose a management credo.

Here are two examples of real management credos from my clients:

A 25-year-old salesper-
son who's about to start as
sales manager:

Management credo
A written set of beliefs that
summarizes your goals as a
manager and the commitments you're
willing to make to get there.

*I want to lead by exam-
ple. If my sales team
sees that I'm honest,
forthright and dedicated, then they'll strive to act the
same. I believe in listening more than talking, and not
trying to have all the answers. I will praise well-earned
success and support employees who need guidance. I
will not accept anything less than full effort from myself
or anyone else.*

A 31-year-old counselor at a nonprofit agency who's about
to start as executive director:

*I believe in taking responsibility for what I can control
and not wasting time with events I cannot control. I will
manage others the way I want to be managed: with
openness and fairness.*
MY GOALS:
1. *To earn everyone's respect.*
2. *To develop each of my employees to reach a higher
   potential.*
3. *To push everyone (including me) so that we don't get
   complacent.*
I COMMIT TO:
1. *Taking bad news well without losing my temper.*
2. *Setting the highest standard of behavior so that
   there's no confusion over what's the right thing to do.*
3. *Remembering to recognize employees' acts of kindness and selflessness.*
4. *Asking for employees' feedback on my performance
   regularly rather than losing touch.*

When you draft your management credo, remember that
you're not trying to please or impress anyone. It's designed as a

private rallying cry, a mission statement that directs your efforts. Write in your own voice and stick to what you believe in most deeply. Probe to uncover why you want to manage people. Your answer should help you compose a credo that you will be more likely to follow.

Your credo should be relatively short, from 50 to 1,000 words. Don't pad it to lend a false sense of depth. It's better not to waste words or repeat yourself.

Choose a format that works for you. As you see from the above examples, one manager broke it down into "My Goals" and "I Commit to" while the other simply wrote out a few sentences and left it at that. Make a numbered list or use bullet points if that will help you express your thoughts.

When you've completed this task, put the draft of your credo aside. Don't even think about it. Then after a few days, take a fresh look at it. Read it all the way through without judging it or making any changes. Let it sink in for another day. Then and only then should you tweak what you've written—and only if you feel it needs revision so it really expresses what you believe, the attitude you want to project, and how you want to lead to get results.

> **⚠ CAUTION!**
>
> **Faking It**
>
> Write your management credo in your own words. Don't try to copy a passage that you've read somewhere else or quote from a leader whom you admire. While it's fine to get inspiration from others, every word of the credo should come from within you. It must be an entirely original, heartfelt expression of your beliefs, your fundamental purpose, and your goals as a manager.

Effective Managing Isn't Easy

As a new manager, you should know that being an effective manager requires a lot of effort. Learning to lead a diverse group of employees can be a harrowing, confounding, and downright painful process.

You should realize what you're getting into by accepting a people management role, and that, at least in the first few months:

- You may not sleep nearly as well at night.
- You'll bring the job home and possibly take out your frustrations on family and friends.
- You'll find yourself putting out fires, despite your best attempts to prevent personnel crises.
- You'll question your judgment when you delegate a task and then find it isn't done well.
- You may lose trust in coworkers when you confide in someone and word leaks out.

In short, expect to feel overwhelmed. That's normal. Almost all new managers tell me that they had no idea how consuming it would be. They often report that "the honeymoon period was so short" or "I had no idea what I was getting into." Usually they're not complaining—just stunned.

I'm not trying to drown you in pessimism. Managing people can be an experience that makes you feel really good about yourself—as long as you understand that it's not a tidy, orderly, predictable

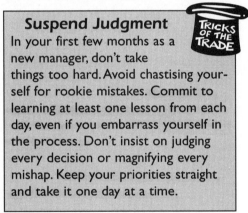

Suspend Judgment

In your first few months as a new manager, don't take things too hard. Avoid chastising yourself for rookie mistakes. Commit to learning at least one lesson from each day, even if you embarrass yourself in the process. Don't insist on judging every decision or magnifying every mishap. Keep your priorities straight and take it one day at a time.

business. Flexibility and maturity will come in handy. So does a dose of good-natured humor that brightens everyone's day.

What's your reward? The best managers often gain more responsibility—fast. More is expected of them, so senior executives tend to raise the bar steadily to see how well these promising supervisors respond to fresh challenges. It can be a heady climb, and big things await those who can overcome early obstacles, bear down, and deliver stellar results.

Just because you're not good friends with your employees doesn't mean relationships no longer matter. The opposite is true. The bonds you establish with your staff serve as the invisible glue that brings everyone together to work toward a common goal.

"Use" Your Employees—Without Making Them Feel Used

New managers sometimes let the rush of authority go to their heads. They suddenly feel awash with entitlement. They start to view themselves as special, different, superior. They may exempt themselves from standard rules of decorum, such as saying "please" or "thank you."

For example, I met a marketing manager, Wes, who was six weeks into his new position. His bosses couldn't understand how Wes had faltered so fast. He had alienated his employees by imposing all kinds of crazy edicts, ranging from an absurdly rigid dress code to having them log their day's work in 15-minute increments on elaborate reporting forms that he designed and distributed. The staff was verging on mutiny.

No Friend of Mine
Draw the line between *manager* and *employee* now, not later. Don't assume just because you've worked alongside buddies in the past that they'll remain friends. The dynamics of the relationship must change now that you're a manager. It's best that everyone remain cordial and professional, but not so friendly that you play favorites or stir jealousies. Your best bet: find your friends somewhere else.

Wes wasn't a villain. He had just lost his bearings. As he put it sheepishly to me, "I guess I got carried away by this whole thing. Being in charge brings out another side of me that even I don't always recognize. Sometimes I think my people are tools to be used to get a job done, and I forget they're actually human beings."

I advised Wes to settle down, draft a management credo, and make corrections in his leadership style. Even though his employees saw him as a micromanaging tyrant, the truth was he had lost his confidence and overcompensated by tightening his grip over his staff.

Even if you keep your ego under wraps as a new manager, you must still find a way to harness your employees' talents to maximum effect. Put crassly, that means using your employees to make you look good. Put not so crassly, it means working together to make the whole group look good because all employees and their manager are succeeding. The effective manager does this wisely and with the full buy-in of employees, rather than exploiting them shamelessly and then hogging the credit for their hard work.

The best way to use employees is to get every-

⚠ CAUTION!

Check Your Ego

Beware of equating strong, gutsy, aggressive management with suffocating your workers in needless directives. If you indulge your sense of self-importance and discount the opinions of others, you will come across as an insecure manager who needs to build himself or herself up at the expense of others. You will alienate the support and willing cooperation of those you manage. In other words, you set yourself up to fail.

thing into the open. Let them know exactly how they're being used. That's right: make it clear what you want from them and why their performance matters. These phrases may help:

- *As a result of your work, we will be able to...*
- *I'm asking you to make a larger contribution by getting the following work done...*
- *Here's a way for us to use your skills more effectively...*

By leveling with your staffers, you make them feel important (not vice versa). Let them know that you need their best effort and they'll feel like valuable team members rather than cogs in a wheel.

If you'll benefit from their hard work, don't keep it a secret. Most employees know full well that they can choose whether to make you look like a genius or a goat. We see examples of this in professional sports. When a basketball team gives up on its coach, the players may slack off because they want to get the coach fired—or they may intentionally foil the coach's plans. If the coach tries to exploit players improperly, the backlash can lead to a humiliating and public termination.

You can avoid such problems with the members of your team by publicly and personally recognizing their efforts and by rewarding them. Show them that you appreciate what they're doing and you'll get better results with less effort. It's the right thing to do—and it's efficient and effective managing.

Exploit Pride, Not Labor

You'll score big wins by getting your employees to push themselves to attain better results. But at the same time, you don't want to turn them into drones who grow overworked and resentful. Solution: let them judge themselves. Have them review their own performance as a prelude to the formal appraisal process where you give your input. Most workers will come down tougher on themselves than you would, thus allowing you to ally yourself with them (whether you agree with their honest self-evaluation or advise them to lighten up).

Testing Your Assumptions

Most new managers assume they know exactly what it takes to thrive in their new position. But jumping to such conclusions can lead them astray.

From my experience advising new managers, here are the three most common assumptions they make:

- The same skills that got me here will help me succeed.
- Employees expect me to have all the answers.
- My employees aren't all that different from me.

Let's hold each of these assumptions up to the light and see what we discover.

Assumption 1: Just Do the Same Thing, but Better

Why were you promoted into management? Don't think for a moment your professional expertise instantly qualifies you to lead others. Sure, you may be a math whiz or a gifted creative thinker. But whatever accolades you've earned based on your specialized knowledge will in no way guarantee that you'll make a great manager.

In fact, your ability to manage people has almost nothing to do with the technical savvy you've gained that has led you to this point in your career. While you may need to train employees and share your wisdom, the more pressing task ahead is to earn their trust and motivate them to perform exceptionally.

It's scary but true: As a new manager, you're starting from scratch. You cannot fall back on whatever got you this far.

Assumption 2: I Must Have All the Answers

One of the hardest lessons for new managers to learn is to say, "I don't know."

If you think your employees will expect you to know everything, you're wrong. They realize you're just doing your job—and your job is to keep an eye on them. When they ask you questions, they may certainly hope for a satisfying answer. But if you don't supply it, they're not going to mock you behind your back or suspect you're an impostor. They'll probably either forget about it or—if they really want an answer—ask someone else.

No manager knows it all. Ironically, some of the best leaders actually know less than their employees about the innards of the business. This ignorance allows them to bring a much-valued fresh perspective to the workplace.

The true test of your managing isn't what you know or don't know. It's how you relate to your employees and how you go about helping them find answers.

Assumption 3: I'll Manage Employees Like I Manage Myself

Here's a news flash that you better process now, not later: your staffers are not reflections of you. They were not made in your image, and they do not have all the same beliefs, biases, and hopes as you.

This may sound obvious. But many managers, flying high on the they're-just-like-me assumption, wind up systematically alienating every one of their employees.

Say you like to play devil's advocate when analyzing an issue. This helps you see both sides before you draw a conclusion. Fair enough.

Yet one of your employees may not appreciate your thought process. In fact, she may view your critical response to her idea as a thinly veiled rejection. She may think you really believe that—that you don't want to give her proposal serious consideration. She won't see it as harmless devil's advocacy; she'll walk away convinced that you just love to knock employees' good ideas, and she may spread the word among her coworkers.

Perhaps you've established a solid track record as a technician. Great. But most of those skills won't necessarily help you handle others. That's an eye-opener for many hotshots who're promoted into management. They figure that they're unstoppable, only to find that all their specialized training doesn't matter much when they go face to face with their staff.

If you must make an assumption, here's a safe one: your employees are all different. They can listen to the same speech and hear different messages. What frightens you might excite them, and what motivates you might bore them.

Acknowledge the diversity among your team. Don't project onto others as you see yourself. The more you can treat each individual separately, the more you'll grow to marvel at the wide range of attitudes and behaviors that your employees bring to work every day.

Manager's Checklist for Chapter 1

❑ Model yourself after star managers. Analyze the keys to their success, and use this as your template.

❑ Gain confidence by becoming more aware—but less judgmental—of how you manage others.

❑ Write a management credo that lists the traits you want to embody and the commitments you're willing to make to succeed.

❑ Expect to be overwhelmed as a new manager. Prepare to pay an early price for success.

❑ Exploit your employees' pride, not their labor. It's fine to use them for your own gain as long as you satisfy their interests, too.

❑ Avoid assumptions that block your ability to manage your employees.

Piercing Six Myths of Management

A s soon as she heard, Sandra called her husband with the great news. "I've just been promoted," she said. "I've been named manager of the data-processing unit!"

Almost immediately, she began to think out loud about how she'd manage. "I'm going to be friends with everyone. I want to break down the barriers between boss and underling. I'm going to decide stuff quickly, not dilly dally over every little thing. I'll run a tight ship and restore order, and I'll stand by my people the way a leader should. Most of all, I'm not taking any guff from anyone. They'll know that what I say goes." This was her view of what good managing is all about.

While Sandra clearly wants to do well, her comments raise a few red flags. She will soon discover that while her views of management certainly sound reasonable, they won't prove all that workable in the real world.

Sandra's not alone. Misconceptions abound when it comes to managing people properly. These false beliefs can befuddle even the most well-intentioned leaders who want to start out on the right foot.

Most new supervisors want it all. They may try to treat their employees as friends while never looking weak or admitting error. They may proudly side with their workers even as they make rash decisions that ignore their staff's concerns. They may order people around without listening, under the impression that leaders must charge ahead without hesitation.

Sandra's not doomed to fail. If she's smart, she will realize in due time that her idealism won't cut it. Experience will teach her to separate the myths from the reality of effective people management.

Myth 1: You Must Call All the Shots

Employees make an average of 100 unsupervised decisions a day. No matter how much power you think you possess as manager, you cannot possibly insert yourself into every situation and play the king or the queen.

Don't believe for a second that just because you're a manager, you're in charge of everything. The fact that you're the boss gives you the right to delegate—to enable others to call the shots on your behalf. By pulling back and putting employees in the driver's seat, you can lead quietly and spread the authority. That's how to build loyalty and teamwork.

Collaboration in Action

When Mike took over as manager, he introduced himself to his employees in a meeting and listed five key staffing decisions he had to make right away. Rather than telegraph his answers or insist that he would study the issues thoroughly and make the right calls, Mike did something unusual: he asked the group to select representatives who could advise him on each of the five areas he needed to evaluate. Thus, the group chose its own panel of experts whom Mike could turn to for input. Mike then collaborated with these five employee advisors to make smart decisions.

The irony of this myth is that no manager in his or her right mind would want to call all the shots. That's a surefire way to a rapid flameout. Viewed strictly in terms of energy, you would be exhausted if you took it upon yourself to make every decision.

Another danger is that you may suffocate your employees. You cannot achieve any collective triumph if you're always at the wheel, never allowing anyone else to steer. If you treat employees like gophers, they'll begin to think like gophers. And you'll be all alone carrying the weight of the world—or at least all the problems that come with your job.

Let's look at how this myth can creep up on an unsuspecting new manager. Say you've just taken over a back-office operation with a dozen file clerks. You figure that to assert your leadership, you need to dive right into the job rather than sit back and wait for crises to arise. So you spend a few days filing charts alongside your lowest-level clerks.

So far, so good. You show your staff you're not too proud to roll up your sleeves and do some grunt work.

But you don't stop there. During your first day in the trenches, you point out what you perceive as inefficiencies. You notice that a clerk keeps affixing new labels onto files that are already clearly marked. And another employee repeatedly wheels over a stepladder so that she can use it to reach a high shelf.

You say to the first clerk, "Hold on. I don't think you need to put new labels on those files. Just leave them alone unless the old label is totally illegible." Then you turn to the other clerk and say, "You keep using a stepladder to do your filing. I'm afraid you'll fall, and even if you don't, that wastes a lot of time getting it into position. I'd like you to file only the first three rows and let a taller employee handle the upper shelves."

You're meddling without even realizing it, calling all the shots when there's no need to say a word. You're not trying to be a pest; in fact, you think that

> ### When to Lay Off
>
> Before you give an order, ask yourself two questions: "What will happen if I wait another week and see what happens?" and "Do I have all the facts I need?" If you keep quiet, maybe your employee can fix what's broken without your involvement. By observing more closely, you may also discover that your order either isn't necessary or would actually make matters worse.

you're actually making the file clerks' job *easier*. You figure that's your job.

But they grumble at your suggestions. They have their reasons for operating the way they do. Some old labels need to be replaced because the company converted certain accounts a few years ago. But a meek clerk may not bother to tell you this key piece of information. And the woman who uses the stepladder knows that she's still the fastest and most organized person in the file room. In the past, she asked taller employees to file on the higher shelves, but she later found too many folders were misfiled. Still, she's too annoyed to correct you, so she complies with your well-meaning—but unsolicited and unwanted—instruction.

Myth 2: You Can't Trust Anyone

Before Julia agreed to become a manager, she sought advice from a grizzled veteran at her firm. When she asked him if she should take the job, he said, "It depends. You're awfully trusting, and that'll get you into trouble. I never trusted my staff. If you blindly trust people, you'll fail."

Julia couldn't believe what she was hearing. She always thought that managers had to trust their employees, at least to some degree. As a trusting soul, she never imagined that the trait would work against her. She didn't think of herself as naïve, just willing to give most people the benefit of the doubt.

In fact, Julia's colleague was perpetuating a destructive management myth. Many managers who embrace the traditional command-and-control model believe that it's foolish to trust employees. The thinking goes, "If I assume every employee is up to no good, I won't be taken advantage of. And if I install enough checks and balances in the system, I can catch wrong-doers quickly and get rid of them."

A corollary of this myth is the mistaken belief that managers must always protect themselves, put themselves first—over the organization's needs and their employees' best interests. Because they've heard that "it's lonely at the top," new managers may decide to spy on their workers excessively and plant gossip that helps them pull the levers in the rumor mill.

I've found a surprising number of rookie managers buy into this myth. Many outwardly warm, friendly professionals carry a cauldron of distrust inside of them, and they actually believe such paranoia will serve them well as managers. In all fairness, however, they know we live in a litigious society. They hear about outrageous lawsuits filed by employees who claim various sorts of discrimination, harassment, and wrongful discharge. They want to keep their guard up, and that vigilance chips away at their willingness to trust.

Refusing to trust anyone won't help you manage more effectively, and you'll certainly isolate yourself. But blind trust is equally dangerous. You need to let your relationships with your employees evolve naturally, realizing that some stumbles will occur along the way. Not everyone can keep a secret, but that doesn't mean you must paint all your workers as loose-lipped blabbermouths. And some new hires will profess their undying loyalty, only to quit when they get a better offer elsewhere. As a manager, you'll learn that trust flows both ways.

> ### Give Trust a Chance
> **Smart Managing**
>
> Here's how to give employees a chance to earn your trust. Call a staffer into your office and close the door. Say, "I'd like you to keep what I'm about to tell you confidential." Then share a few harmless, noncontroversial bits of news that you reveal to no one else. Wait a few weeks and monitor the grapevine. If word spreads, at least you know whom *not* to trust. While this test isn't foolproof, it's a good starting point to screen employees.

Myth 3: You Must Remain Objective at All Times

During World War II, many Americans idolized the dry-eyed, stone-faced foreign correspondents who reported from Europe. They were seen as gutsy, tough-as-nails journalists who could keep their composure when engulfed by brutal fighting and bloody bombing runs.

Today, many new managers buy into the same myth. Like a would-be Edward R. Murrow, the typical supervisor may try to come across as a steely, expressionless fighter who's unfazed by the craziness that surrounds him.

As much as you may want to act like a cool-under-fire leader, too much coolness can strip away your natural personality. There's no rule that requires managers to act like robots, bouncing from task to task without showing any trace of emotion. In fact, your eagerness to play the part of *Star Trek*'s Mr. Spock—all calm and rational—can backfire. You'll lose countless opportunities to connect with your team and inspire them to reach greater heights.

In your first few months as manager, you may go out of your way to "sound serious." You may hold in your laugh or refuse to crack a joke to enliven a discussion. You may greet an employee's enthusiasm with stony silence, thinking that it would be immature or imprudent to get carried away. When someone looks shaken or cries in your presence, you may offer some tissues stoically and then pretend it doesn't affect you in the least.

Beware: All this android-like behavior won't help you manage people any better. You want to appear strong and resilient, but you'll appear heartless and detached. You want to set an example of hardened determination, but you'll come across as a manager blinded by tunnel vision and unable to empathize with others.

There's a time and a place for remaining objective, of course, as long as you don't overdo it. If you're shifting into data-gathering mode, you'll want to collect information

---

Sound Like You Mean It

Your communication style at work should not differ all that much from the way you chat with friends and family. Here's how to make sure you're not lapsing into an emotionless monotone. Tape yourself the next time you give a presentation or lead a staff meeting. Play back your tape to a good friend who knows you outside of work. Ask if you sound any different. Ideally, your friend should recognize your workplace personality as consistent with how you sound all the time.

dispassionately without judging it. This would be the case, for example, when you investigate an employee's complaint, experiment with different solutions to a thorny problem, or analyze results from customer surveys.

Similarly, when you must say "no" to an employee, base your answer on facts rather than emotions. You'll find it easier to muster the courage to come down hard if you've aligned plenty of concrete evidence to support your position. You can reinforce your firm no-means-no answer by sticking to hard data—without allowing your emotions to surface. Losing your hard-nosed objectivity can prolong the decision-making process. Employees can sense that you're subject to an emotional appeal, and they may repeat their requests while tugging at your heart strings.

Myth 4: You Must Defend Your Staff

Ron's boss didn't sound happy. She summoned him into her office, closed the door, and started to chastise him for his lackadaisical supervision of his customer-service staff.

"Your people don't even answer the phone on the fourth ring," she said. "And when they finally say, 'Hello,' they sound bored and listless. I even heard one of them sigh—loudly—into the phone. I felt like I was being a pest, when all I was doing was asking for directions. You've got to do a better job training these people and watching them to make sure they perform up to our standards."

Ron instinctively did what he thought he had to do: defend his staff. He excused them for sounding harassed, but they're "overworked because we're short-staffed." He explained that many customers who ask for directions hang up in frustration because they have trouble following so many steps, so his employees "understandably dread this task." He said that with the air conditioning broken, his customer-service reps were hot and irritable over the last week, which contributed to their phone manner.

Regardless of what you think of Ron's points, you should realize by now that he did not have to stand up for his employees' poor performance. His boss wasn't asking for excuses or explanations; she wanted the problem fixed, period. Ron's insistence on defending his staff only made her angrier and lowered her estimation of Ron's managerial ability.

You can tell that you're clinging to this myth if you start to take any criticism of your staff personally. You may react impulsively to any hint that they're not pulling their weight. In extreme cases, you may lose perspective and glorify your employees as unsung heroes who can do no wrong.

A big part of managing others is learning to separate your own performance from theirs. If they let you down or prove ineffectual, despite your efforts to train them, that's life. Your employees may simply fail and your bosses may not like what they see. That's unavoidable, so prepare for it. Defend them only when you're sure it's justified.

It's fine to stick up for people who are unfairly accused or judged harshly by others in the organization who lack accurate information. But you should never grow so attached to your team that you rush to defend their every move without first assessing the merits of what you hear.

> **Tricks of the Trade**
>
> **Talk Less, Extract More**
>
> The next time you're tempted to defend your staff from a boss's or colleague's attack, try this strategy. Listen without interrupting. Wait patiently for the speaker to unload all of his or her concerns or criticisms about your employees. Don't rush to respond; instead, pose a few follow-up questions to gather more information. Or simply ask for examples. The advantage of this is twofold: you avoid falling into the trap of providing an instant defense *and* you show you're the kind of mature manager who can face unwelcome news head-on and dig for additional facts.

Myth 5: You Cannot Back Down

If you grew up having to fend off bullies, perhaps you learned one of the harsh lessons of the schoolyard: the only way to win a brawl is to remain the last one standing. Backing down equals humiliation.

Fortunately, the same rules don't apply in the workplace. In fact, to stay out of fights and give up ground to a more forceful opponent is sometimes your smartest move. But some fresh-faced managers may recall their days on the playground, when taking punch after punch was better than walking away, and conclude that they must never, ever give an inch.

I find many supervisors mistakenly think that once they stake out a position, they must prove that they're right at all costs. Or they may go out of their way to prove that they're in charge by refusing to apologize, admit error, or revisit an issue that they've already attempted to resolve. It's a myth that they seem to embrace enthusiastically, because it gives them a sense of power and infallibility. Even if their conscience tells them to reverse course, they can rest easy knowing that, as the boss, they're supposed to take a firm stand and not budge.

Here are six situations when you have more to gain by disregarding this dangerous myth and backing down than by trying to play the role of a stubborn fighter:

- **You state the wrong facts.** When you base a decision on incorrect information, there's nothing to gain by clinging to your conclusion. Your staff won't lose any respect for you if you acknowledge the truth in a forthright manner. Even if you've already given orders that you now must withdraw or modify, it's better to do that than to keep quiet and let the damage spread.
- **You're fighting for peanuts.** If you're negotiating a million-dollar contract, it's obviously unwise to backpedal at the first sign of resistance. But if a conflict erupts over how you intend to punish an employee for an unexcused 10-minute absence during an otherwise quiet day, then you're going to squander precious goodwill to "win" a minor skirmish. Other employees will take notice and view your every move with suspicion.

- **Circumstances change.** New managers should stand their ground when they want to prove a point and showcase their leadership. But if events unfold unpredictably and it's no longer worth fighting the battle, then it's silly to withstand the forces of change. Example: You don't want to back down after putting an employee on probation for violating the dress code, despite protestations from other workers. But then your company's president announces a new policy: every day is now "casual day," with looser guidelines regarding clothing. Now you have a convenient "out," so take it.

- **Precedent saves you.** If other managers in your organization have backed down when faced with a similar challenge—and survived to tell about it—then you're safe following their lead. This often happens when an incoming manager tries to enact stricter forms of discipline, only to unleash a staff rebellion. Then the news spreads that another manager who tried the same tough strategy wound up compromising with employees over what types of discipline would ultimately apply. You can save face by telling your employee, "I'm willing to be flexible here because we have a precedent for handling this" or "I'll compromise because it's part of our corporate culture to work together to resolve these kind of issues."

- **Your boss disapproves.** A great reason to stand firm is to prove to your higher-ups that you're determined to make waves and manage more boldly than your predecessors. While that's a worthy goal, make sure you'll truly impress your boss with your show of spine. If you report to a boss whose style is conciliatory, however, then watch out! Your refusal to back down can work against you.

- **Great results hang in the balance.** As a new manager, you cannot sacrifice bottom-line results in the name of winning a juvenile game of "chicken." Backing down can work to your advantage if it enables you and your team to resume your work and achieve an important objective. The benefits of managing your staff to produce a resounding success—whether in terms of cost savings, productivity gains, or other high-visibility triumphs—easily outweigh the cost of retreating when you'd prefer to hold your ground.

These six scenarios do not represent an exhaustive list of all the times when it's smart to back down. As situations arise, you must examine your intent. Do you want to prove a point at all costs, even if it means alienating your employees or even colleagues and bosses? Or do you want to display toughness by knowing when to fold your cards so that you win larger prizes in the future?

Myth 6: You're the Best Teacher

In exposing this myth, you need to accept one undeniable fact: you don't know everything.

Just because you're given a staff to manage doesn't make you their one and only teacher. You're not supposed to spoon-feed them knowledge so that they know everything that you know. As much as you may want to sit down with each employee and go over certain processes and procedures, you can't clone your know-how and pass it around like sticks of gum.

You're one of many sources of insight for your employees. That should give you a sense of relief. For starters, they'll learn from each other by osmosis. They'll absorb tips and techniques to work smarter simply through teaming up. They may also extract pointers from other executives, team leaders, and outside consultants.

This doesn't mean you should teach them just the basic skills and then back off and let the rest take care of itself. You still need to create a learning environment and encourage employees to share ideas and teach each other. A useful way to plant the seeds of knowledge is to designate certain individuals to train others in a specific area. Examples: You send Jim to a database management course so that he in turn can help his coworkers understand this process, and you help Mary understand risk management so that she in turn can spread the word on worker safety and accident prevention. By turning key employees into experts, you can create a teaching corps so that the members of your team essentially educate each other.

> **Key Term**
>
> **Train the trainer** A program usually led by consultants in which selected employees are shown how to train their coworkers in specified areas by undergoing formal training to become experts. They're then able to pass their new knowledge on to others. They're given a package of printed support materials—such as instructor notes, a participant workbook, and handouts—so that they're now ready to lead training sessions on their own.

While you're not the best (or only) teacher for your employees, you can take steps to increase the amount of learning that takes place. Begin by encouraging your team to ask penetrating questions. At staff meetings, don't feel obliged to answer every one of their inquiries. Throw open the discussion and let participants bounce ideas off each other. Ideally, you want them to engage in their own search for answers, to exchange information and observations.

Don't worry if such discussions veer off on tangents. The best teachers don't necessarily teach in the conventional sense; they just sit back and guide others to dig for answers.

Another way to spread knowledge is to invite experts in to address your employees. These experts can come from other departments within your company or from the outside. Let them relate their experiences and findings on a topic to enlighten your workers. Choose subjects that your team has asked you about in the past; this shows that you're responsive to their needs and supportive of their interest in learning.

If you embrace the myth that you're the best teacher for your employees, then you may fall into the trap of spouting platitudes and pretending to know more than you really do. What's worse, your team may tire of your pontificating and

Lunch 'n' Learn

To foster a more lively learning environment, a new manager launched "lunch 'n' learn" sessions in his company's cafeteria. On the last Thursday of every month, employees were invited to gather during their lunch break and listen to experts discuss a job-related skill. During the first six sessions, speakers covered topics ranging from public speaking tips to time management. The manager recruited local consultants to speak, offering them a free lunch and a chance to "rehearse" in front of company officials who might hire them in the future. Thus, the cost of the manager's program was minimal. And as word spread of these stimulating sessions, turnout soared.

question your credibility. When workers start to doubt the accuracy of your remarks or dread your "lectures," then you know you're overdoing it.

Remember: your job as manager isn't to teach employees everything they need to know. By letting them find their own way, you wind up with a more motivated, intelligent team.

Manager's Checklist for Chapter 2

❑ Limit the decisions you make so that you delegate more responsibility to your staff.

❑ While it's unwise to blindly believe everything your employees tell you, give them chances to earn your trust.

❑ Radiate enthusiasm and express genuine feelings when appropriate. Don't bury your personality because you think managers cannot show emotion.

❑ Stand by your staff when the situation calls for it, but don't instinctively defend them from any and all criticism.

❑ Assess whether it's in your interest to back down rather than cling to an untenable position.

❑ Give employees ample opportunities to learn from others rather than try to be their sole teacher.

How to Build Momentum in a New Job

Congratulations! You've been promoted. It's your first day as a new manager. You're wearing your best outfit, your hair is freshly cut, and you're ready to lead your staff to greatness.

You want to start on the right foot. Other managers have warned you that first impressions matter, so you want to make every effort to establish the right relationship with your employees from Day One. You also know that if you can gain credibility quickly, you'll find it easier to give instructions that others will follow.

It makes you nervous to think about it, but it's true: you're now under a microscope. Your employees—as well as your boss—will be very attentive to your words and actions and judging you by them. As the cops tell suspects, anything you say can and will be used against you.

Consistency Counts

The best way to build momentum as a new manager is to make it clear to everyone what you stand for. Then be sure to *follow through.* Employees cannot help but respect a boss who begins by communicating a few core principles—and then exemplifies those principles in the weeks and months ahead.

That's why a management credo helps. As we discussed in Chapter 1, by preparing a short summary of what you believe as a manager, you're less likely to fumble for direction as you get to know your employees. With a written credo as your reference point, you can always remind yourself of the big picture: what you're trying to accomplish and how you intend to get the job done.

By showing from the outset that you're guided by unshakable, unassailable underlying beliefs, you eliminate much of the ambiguity and confusion that employees often resent in new managers. Workers often complain to me of supervisors who suddenly start acting like politicians as soon as they're put in charge of a staff.

You'll squander any traces of initial goodwill by trying to feed everyone what they want to hear or spouting platitudes about the kind of unit you want to run. Employees see through such meaningless drivel. They want straight answers. You make matters worse by pretending to know more than you do—or trying to overcompensate by appearing so confident that you border on arrogant and infallible.

In the opening weeks of your new job, it's important not to send contradictory signals or give different answers to the same question. That's a common rookie mistake. You'll stumble out of the gate if your employees approach you in an exasperated tone and say, "You said something else yesterday" or "I'm not sure if you've

> **Wimping Out** ⚠️ CAUTION!
>
> Most employees respond well to straight-talking managers. If you repeatedly respond to their concerns with mushy or evasive answers such as "Let's revisit that later," "We'll see," or "I'll try my hardest," you'll bob and weave your way into oblivion. It's fine to say, "I don't know," as long as you ask some fact-gathering questions and show interest in formulating a serious answer. That's the kind of consistency they'll appreciate.

approved or denied my request." To avoid this, follow these three rules:

1. **Don't improvise when you can repeat yourself.** Give simple answers to employees' questions, without inserting lots of asides. Also provide the identical response as many times as necessary, even if two workers rephrase a similar question when they ask you. Don't feel obliged to editorialize or give new shadings to statements you've already made to others on the same topic.

2. **Don't oversell or overpromise.** Learn to consistently underpromise and overdeliver. That's better than hyping your latest proposal, only to change your mind in a flash. Whenever you speculate about the future with your employees, err on the conservative side. Make modest commitments you're sure you can keep; then, if you wind up exceeding others' expectations, you'll be a hero or heroine.

3. **Don't fake it.** Never speak authoritatively on a subject you know little or nothing about. That sounds obvious, but many new managers dread having to admit what they don't know in the early weeks on the job. But there's no better way to build credibility than to acknowledge your limits and show a willingness to learn along with your employees.

A final point about consistency: don't play favorites. If you take over a management job where you're tempted to treat your longtime friends differently from everyone else, you're doomed to fail. Treat every individual the same. Drill home the same messages, give the same answers, and express the same goals regardless of which employee you're addressing.

Love at First Sight?

"I'll make one promise," said Sam as he introduced himself to his staff on his first day. "I'm always going to treat each of you the way I want to be treated. Let me tell you why: it's not that I'm a warm and fuzzy guy. No, the real reason is that one day you may be my boss, and payback's a bummer."

The room erupted in laughter. Sam had his employees in the palm of his hand.

By making a favorable first impression with your employees, you make everything that follows much easier. You give yourself a wider margin for error later, because you persuade your people that you're a decent, fair-minded manager. Ideally, you want to leave your first meeting with your team by having them nod and say to one another, "Now *that's* a manager I can work for."

In the above remark, Sam pulls it off brilliantly. By stating one of his core principles in a humorous way, he achieves three goals:

1. He shows he doesn't take himself too seriously.
2. He implicitly compliments his employees by implying that they're talented enough to be his boss one day.
3. He makes a solemn promise without wasting words, thus magnifying the importance of his commitment.

Like Sam, you want to win over your staff from the beginning. With careful planning, you can make all the right moves.

Preparing for the First Meeting

If you want to get off to a running start with your employees, here are three words of advice: don't wing it. Plan every detail so that you create a supportive, nonthreatening atmosphere.

Even if you've met some of your staff individually, it's the first team meeting that sets the tone and serves as your true initiation. By making everyone feel comfortable, you build instant momentum and instill confidence in your leadership. Such meetings should occur on your first day, not a week or two into your job.

Prepare by making a list of questions that your employees may ask you. Include issues that individuals have already raised with you one on one. Plan responses to each question, noting key points you want to express. Test yourself by rehearsing your answers—ideally by reciting them into a tape recorder—and running them through a battery of tests:

- Did I say what I wanted to say?

- Did I use words and phrases that my employees will understand?
- Did I communicate clearly and concisely?

If you answer yes to all three questions, you're ready to proceed with confidence.

If possible, reserve a cozy conference room where everyone must sit near one another. That fosters a more close-knit feeling. If people are too scattered or retreat into their own space or form "camps," you'll find it harder to rally them as a group. Plus, making eye contact is easier if people sit closer to you.

If you're nervous, don't fight it. Trying to hide your opening-day jitters won't work. Instead, accept your fears as a healthy sign that you want to do well. Tell yourself, "The fact that I'm anxious tells me that I care about this job." The less you dwell on your nerves, the more you can occupy yourself with other, more pressing concerns—like connecting with your staff.

> **MISTAKE PROOFING**
>
> **Circle the Troops**
> Arrange the seats in a circle so that all participants are positioned as peers, including you. A classroom-style setting can create an invisible barrier between you and your staff, because the rows of seats may make employees feel like students (and they'll perceive you as the teacher/taskmaster). Same goes with a U-shaped conference setup with you at the head of the table.

For example, it's common for new managers on their first day to get caught up in relatively minor worries, such as how they look or whether they remember everyone's name. Rid yourself of such petty concerns by taking some practical preventive steps. Choose the appropriate outfit a week in advance and make sure it's freshly cleaned and ironed. And ask your human-resources manager for a list of your employees' names ahead of time—along with a photo and some brief biographical information—so that you can get a head start on getting to know them.

Don't call attention to your anxiety on your first day. If you flub the first few lines of your introductory speech, move on;

avoid apologizing and starting over from the beginning. If you make a *faux pas*, such as not hearing someone's name and calling them by the wrong name, laugh easily and recover in a flash.

Remember: your employees will be nervous, too. They'll want to make a good first impression on you, too. They may sense you're a bit nervous, but they won't mind as long as you don't make a big deal about it. What *will* bother them is if they perceive that you're going out of your way to be mean or tough or somehow fake. The more authentic you appear, the better.

During this first meeting with your staff, resist the urge to volunteer too much information about yourself. Your short introduction should consist of no more than the basics: your name, prior job, and overriding goal for your team. Rehearse this mini-speech in the days before your first day; if it's longer than three minutes, cut it.

When you invite your employees to speak, don't keep tugging the conversation back to *you*. Some new managers arrive on their first day full of doubt and insecurity, and they relieve their angst by trying to play "topper" and bragging about their accom-

> ### Hello, My Name Is ...
> **Smart Managing**
>
> Begin the meeting by introducing yourself briefly. Then ask employees to introduce themselves by mentioning a particular skill that they bring to their job. Tell them not to mention their present or past job titles, which can interfere with unity and imply power and seniority. As you go around the room, don't interrupt the speakers. But ask clarifying questions as needed, such as "How did you develop that skill?"

plishments every few minutes. That's a surefire way to pummel your employees into submission, rather than build momentum and excite your team about your leadership.

Score Quick Wins

In the course of your first meeting with employees and subsequent one-on-one discussions, you should begin to identify the problems they care about most. This information tells you where to focus your efforts to produce early results.

I, Me, Mine

You'll know that you're hogging the spotlight if you spend your first meeting talking about your experiences and spouting your opinions. Keep the personal reflections to a minimum, unless you're asked point-blank by an employee to share your views on a particular topic (and that's rare). Strive to limit your speaking to 10% of the meeting, thus allowing your employees to take center stage and bounce off each other's remarks.

There's no better way to establish momentum as a new manager than to show that you're responsive to your team's concerns. If they complain about the company's rigid bureaucracy, find a way to loosen up. If they confess that they're exhausted from overwork—and you conclude they're putting in far too many hours—relieve their burden by hiring more people, getting some temps in, or temporarily tackling some of the overflow work yourself, while working on ways to reduce the load. If they need certain equipment to perform their jobs better, make every effort to acquire these tools quickly.

Here are some other ways to form solid relationships with employees and thus prolong your honeymoon period:

1. **Remove longstanding irritants.** The longer something has plagued your employees, the more heroic you'll appear if you address it. As a new manager, you cannot be blamed for anything that predated your arrival. So in many cases you have nothing to lose by trying to play fixer when they propose reasonable solutions. Example: If customer service reps tell you they've repeatedly asked for private voice mail to respond to clients faster, make it happen. If your bosses sit on your request, implement it on your own. Employees love having can-do mavericks for managers. But be prudent here and make sure your actions are on solid ground and adding real value to the organization.

2. **Simplify their lives.** Find a way to make your employees' jobs easier. Examples: eliminate a needless procedure, give them more flexibility over their hours, reduce the number of forms they need to complete.

3. **Assign team leaders to recommend solutions.** Convening a team every time your employees mention a problem can get you into trouble, especially if you're not ready to act on their suggestions. But in your first weeks on the job, you can use this approach effectively. Avoid acting like a politician who's scared of making a tough decision, by distributing a precise timetable to each team leader (who's chosen by teammates, not by you). Present dates when you want to see a list of proposed solutions *and* commit to a date when you promise to respond. Then follow through.

In your eagerness to please your new staff, beware of giving too much away. Employees who think you're a pushover may take advantage of your kindness by upping the ante. The more you do for them, the more they might ask. Then you're stuck in a never-ending spiral of granting concessions, approving expenditures, and compromising your objectives to accommodate employees' whims.

The whole point of scoring quick wins is to generate momentum and assert your leadership. You must still choose your battles and guard against overindulging your employees. If you give them too much, too soon, you will set yourself up to fail over the long run.

Unclog "Input Channels"

After their first month, I like to ask new managers to describe in one word their experience so far. The No. 1 answer: alone.

They often tell me that as much as they think they're off to a good start, they have no idea how they're doing. They cannot confide in a staff member, because they fear they won't get a straight answer. And their hands-off boss may not pay much attention or offer much encouragement in the early weeks. That leaves these fledgling managers to shrug and assume they're doing OK, without gathering input from others.

To avoid falling into a black hole of uncertainty, you need to flood yourself with feedback from all sides. That probably won't happen on its own. When you're new on the job and you stumble out of the gate, you may not even realize that anything's amiss unless someone tells you. In blissful ignorance, you may figure that everything's fine. Then you're stunned to learn that your staff is lining up against you and your boss plans to demote you.

To prevent this, you need *input channels.* By collecting helpful feedback from your staff on how you're doing, you can make adjustments before it's too late.

Input channels Ways in which you can get feedback from your employees on your performance as a manager. Examples include informal team meetings, formal evaluations, a monthly grading, and an anonymous suggestion box.

To establish input channels, you must make it easy for your employees to give you their input. Most subordinates will not give you a running commentary on your performance. Even if you ask them for feedback, they may not necessarily provide the kind of revealing, honest answers you want.

Here are three ways to probe for information on how you're doing:

1. **Formalize the process.** Distribute simple, one-page feed-back forms on a regular basis to your staff, such as at biweekly staff meetings. Invite them to tell you in writing how they perceive your managing style. Give them a chance to rate your performance in key areas, such as assigning a 1-to-5 grade to your ability to motivate, willingness to listen, responsiveness to their needs, and the level of support you give them. By allowing them to type their responses or send you an e-mail from a shared PC, you can assure them their comments will remain anonymous. *Warning*: Never collect the forms right away. Employees will assume you can identify their handwriting, and this will inhibit them.

2. **Seek casual advice.** In the first few months as a manager, show plenty of interest in your employees' ideas and opinions. The more you get them to share their thoughts, the

more likely they'll open up to you about your performance. Say, "You've given me a lot to think about, but one area we haven't discussed is your impression so far of my management style. Can you give me some input?"

3. **Trace changes in behavior.** As you get to know your employees, watch how they relate to you. Note their body language. Do they smile and seem comfortable chatting with you? Do they volunteer comments when they run into you in the hall? Do they station themselves near you in a meeting or try to keep a low profile? Armed with these observations, monitor changes in the first month or two on the job. If you notice someone no longer seems as eager to stop and chat in the lunchroom, for instance, you may want to get input as to why.

To unclog input channels, prepare to listen without lashing out. Accept that you may hear things that surprise and upset you. But rather than react negatively, maintain your equanimity. This way, you condition your employees to "tell it like it is" without fear of recrimination or backlash.

I'm always reminding new managers that the input they get from employees is priceless, whether they like to hear it or not. By absorbing it in a

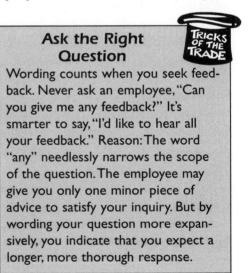

Ask the Right Question

Wording counts when you seek feedback. Never ask an employee, "Can you give me any feedback?" It's smarter to say, "I'd like to hear all your feedback." Reason: The word "any" needlessly narrows the scope of the question. The employee may give you only one minor piece of advice to satisfy your inquiry. But by wording your question more expansively, you indicate that you expect a longer, more thorough response.

graceful manner, they guard against self-delusion. They'll never let their performance sink too deep as long as they're aware of what needs to improve.

The worst response is defensiveness. You'll crush any momentum you try to build by trying to explain yourself excessively instead of simply listening to the input you solicit.

Give Me More

Dave's employees freely told him how they felt about his management approach. From the day he started as manager, he vowed to treat every piece of input as a gold nugget. When he asked for feedback, he took unpleasant news with good cheer by thinking, "I'm so lucky to learn this now, not later." When employees mentioned issues that Dave deemed unfair or beyond his control, he thought, "It's not their job to tell me how to correct my performance, just to share their honest thoughts with me." After his employees gave input, Dave automatically would reply, "Thank you. Please, go on." And, thanks to his gentle prodding, they would say even more.

The more input channels you establish, the more prudent risks you'll take. If you know how your employees perceive you, that can give you the confidence to have them experiment with new ways to work. You'll also lead more dynamically if you're aware of what your team likes and doesn't like about how you communicate and motivate them.

If you fail to get feedback, then you can start off on the wrong foot and tumble downhill from there. You want to generate that head of steam, but nothing seems to work. You may begin to sense that you're struggling, so you fall into the rookie manager trap of resting on your laurels. You retreat into what you know best: your technical strengths or professional expertise. But now that you're a manager, those skills no longer will save you. You need to expand your repertoire by finding new people-management tools, not just relying on what worked when you were on your own.

Are You Ready for Anything?

Nothing kills momentum like a flaring crisis. It can arise out of nowhere and deplete everyone's energy for days at a time.

While you cannot possibly put out every fire before it ignites, you can take steps to reduce the risk. This requires a high level of readiness. By anticipating what can go wrong and devising a strategy to guard against it, you impose at least some order on an otherwise disorderly universe of work-related mishaps.

When you first get promoted into management, schedule meetings with other managers who've had the job you're about to take. If you're ascending into a newly designed job with no predecessors, interview individuals who hold similar positions either inside or outside your organization.

Use these meetings to get acquainted with the types of challenges you can expect to confront in the early going. Ask questions such as:

- In your first six months in that job, what was your biggest surprise?
- What was the worst crisis you ever faced in the job? What was the worst crisis in the first six months?
- If you wish you could have known one thing about the job before you took it, what would that be?
- What steps did you take early on that helped minimize problems down the line? What steps do you wish you had taken?

As you gather answers, you can begin to spot potential trouble spots. A seasoned manager may warn you not to trust the weekly activity reports or to devote at least a few hours a week keeping key colleagues "in the loop." If managers in another department tend to feel ignored or taken for granted, for example, they may not cooperate as much and make your life harder once you take over. Knowing this now can give you a heads-up on how to manage more effectively from Day One.

Aside from picking the brains of veteran managers, don't forget your boss. Realize, however, that the executive to whom you

Meeting of the Managers

A great way to anticipate crises that can derail your early progress is to arrange a meeting with at least three respected, experienced managers who're familiar with the job you're about to start. Ask them what kinds of pitfalls may lurk ahead for you. After launching the discussion, let the participants respond to each other's comments; don't overfacilitate. Most managers will enjoy the chance to share war stories and find out how they handled the same kind of problems.

report won't necessarily have hands-on awareness of the kinds of fires that can flare in your new job. Many executives are somewhat removed from the daily operational realities of management positions, although they might not want to admit that.

In any case, inform your boss that you want to hit the ground running as a new manager, ready to avoid any crises from the start. Solicit advice and try to uncover problems that can erupt soon after you start.

As an added precaution, submit a list of challenges that you expect to face in your new job. Review this list with your boss. Examples might include "train employees to use new computer system" or "negotiate new contracts with suppliers." As you discuss each item, work with your boss to identify what can go wrong and what preventive steps you can take. Your boss won't necessarily give you all the answers, but may at least guide you to approach potential crises in a calm, sensible manner and think of ways to reduce your risk.

Smart Managing

Ask Hypothetical Questions

Occasionally ask your employees, "Are you prepared for...?" and "What would you do if...?" questions. Just don't overdo it. If you sound like a Cassandra who's obsessed with dark days to come, your prudent disaster planning may be misinterpreted by your employees as undue pessimism or lack of faith in their abilities. But such questions—when posed judiciously—can train your team to respond well to crises and extinguish fires before they rage out of hand.

Finally, train your employees to anticipate problems and address them in advance. Explain to them that some fires cannot be prevented, and you will need to save all of your team's energy and resourcefulness to put out the flames. Then add that it's vital to get ready now for those problems that you and your staff *can* control and reduce the odds of needless hassles later.

To increase everyone's preparedness, ask your employees what kind of crises they have found the most disruptive before you arrived. Most workers love to talk about what can go wrong, and they may give you ample suggestions on how to plan for worst-case scenarios.

If they don't have that many tales of woe and hardship from the past, try asking them, "What crisis do you fear the most?" This may unleash a few doom-and-gloom comments, but that's what you want. Ideally, you should come away with a much better understanding of the kind of snafus that can destroy the progress that you and your staff intend to make in the months ahead.

Manager's Checklist for Chapter 3

❑ Send clear, consistent signals in your early months as manager. Express your core principles and key goals and stick to them.

❑ If you don't know something, admit it. Employees will appreciate your honesty and you'll earn credibility.

❑ Make a strong first impression by holding a staff meeting on your first day as manager. Leave plenty of time for employees to introduce themselves and discuss their strengths.

❑ Chalk up a quick win that endears you to your employees. Examples include removing a much-hated bureaucratic process or arranging for workers to have better tools or equipment.

❑ Make it easy for your employees to give you feedback. Give them many ways to communicate their input to you—and then respond to it gracefully.

❑ Put out fires before they begin by anticipating what can go wrong and devising appropriate strategies.

Managing to Listen

L ast week, a regulatory compliance officer at a bank called to tell me she was just named manager of her unit. She could barely contain her excitement.

"This means people are finally going to listen to me," she said. "When I make recommendations or point out problems, it's not like I'll be talking to myself any more. And I have a lot to say, believe me. This is great: I'll have more of an impact because what I say goes."

I didn't want to rain on her parade, but I had to warn her that it's more important to *listen* than to *speak*, especially as she settles into her new job. Many first-time managers think that it's now up to them to do most of the talking. As subordinates, they had to take orders or quietly sit and nod while a bigwig babbled. They paid their dues by biting their lip and pretending not to mind when a boss monopolized their time by telling long, boastful stories. As new managers, they may figure it's their turn to talk—to make up for lost time sitting in silence.

Many people equate listening with subservience and speaking with authority. That can lead managers to talk louder and more forcefully than everyone else in the room. They can grow attached to the sound of their own voice, convinced that they've reached the promised land where they can repeat themselves at will, crack their favorite jokes, and interrupt underlings with impunity.

In fact, your listening skills count even more now that you're in charge. Your ability to observe others and extract valuable information from them will help you persuade them. Your willingness to stay attentive even when you're tired or distracted will help you build trust. And your commitment to interpret and assess what you hear, rather than just capture it at face value, will save you from costly misunderstandings.

By establishing a baseline of how you listen, you can identify barriers to clear communication. This awareness enables you to take steps to overcome your vulnerabilities so that you become a stronger, more resilient listener.

Check all statements that describe how you communicate:

- ❏ I'm more of a talker than a listener.
- ☑ I find it harder to listen when I become highly emotional.
- ❏ I often find myself faking it, pretending to listen while I'm really thinking about other things.
- ☑ I usually try to listen while I think of what I want to say next.
- ❏ I'm a selective listener: I pay more attention to speakers whom I respect.
- ☑ My mind wanders almost immediately when I must listen to a babbler.
- ☑ I often interrupt people who repeat themselves.

Each of the statements that you checked indicates a potential trouble spot. But don't worry that you're doing anything "bad" or "wrong." Many of the new managers I train tend to fret if they check three or four of the above items. They assume that they're hopelessly weak listeners who need remedial help. Rest assured it's common for people to recognize some if not all of these statements. The key is to build on this awareness-raising exercise and find strategies to sharpen your listening skills.

Let's get started.

Tapping the Power of Silence

Many managers admit that they're poor listeners. They confess to me that if they could just keep their mouth shut, they would build better rapport with their employees, stop themselves from making mistaken assumptions, and avoid jumping to conclusions.

They tell me how badly they listen—over and over again! They often subject me to rambling monologues in which they berate themselves for sloppy listening. After making their point abundantly clear, they pause to take a breath and ask me, "Does this make any sense?"

"Oh, yeah," I nod. "I see the problem."

In short, they don't know when to stop. They lapse into "motor mouth mode," stringing their words together to create an oral traffic jam with no apparent end.

It's not enough to acknowledge that you could improve how you listen. The first step on the road to improvement is simple: keep quiet.

Using silence well doesn't automatically make you a better listener. After all, you can daydream while pretending to pay attention to your employees' comments. But if you're trying to guide staffers to think for themselves—rather than look to you for instant answers—then your silence will show that you're willing to wait and hear what they have to say. By sitting still without constantly hogging the conversation, you send a message that you're not going to do the mental work for them.

This works particularly well when you're helping

Apply the Breaks

The next time you're about to interrupt a speaker, don't. Take a break. Force yourself to clam up. To ensure you don't cut someone off, silently count to three before you respond. That way, you insert a cushion of silence into the conversation. At that point, don't be surprised if the speaker chimes in again. You can often learn the most revealing facts from your employees only *after* you stay silent an extra few moments. An employee who's hiding something may spill the beans if you don't rush to interrupt.

an employee make a tough decision. Rookie managers can construct an airtight argument and list dozens of superb reasons why they think a worker should act a certain way. But that won't necessarily sway an ambivalent person. You may need to let the individual talk it out to grow truly convinced of the proper course of action.

The worst listeners use words as weapons. They may assume that if they can drown employees in facts, opinions, or examples, they will overcome their team's objections and gain compliance. The truth is the reverse: it's by pouring on the silence that you enable others to decide that you're right.

When you're managing employees, remember that it's up to them to decide what to do. If you order them around indefinitely, you'll turn them into mindless drones. That means you need to use patience and eye contact, rather than firing off a fusillade of commands. Plus, you'll exert more influence by allowing them to speak freely. Don't feel obliged to reply to everything they say. Just let them think out loud and show silent, intent interest.

It's Sure Quiet in Here

When Rajat Gupta, the head of McKinsey & Co., made a presentation to a large corporation about the need to manage change, the client questioned if all the expected turmoil was worth the risk. Gupta did not launch into a sales pitch trying to prove to the client why his proposals made sense, according to a story in *Business Week*. Instead, he kept quiet. "He just looked them right in the eyes," said a McKinsey colleague who was there. "A minute must have passed in silence. It was quite effective, because the client had to make the decision. It wasn't ours to make."

What's to Learn?

Many professional athletes insist that their success is "all mental." Superstars such as basketball's Michael Jordan and baseball's Mark McGwire have discussed the role of raw will and concentration in improving their performance.

Same goes when you want to listen better. There's no substitute for focus and mental discipline. If you're not listening as raptly as you'd like, the problem boils down to the fact that you're giving yourself permission to tune out. The real test is whether you can bear down and concentrate on what others tell you, even if it takes Herculean effort.

To train yourself to be more attentive, you need to step back and remind yourself *why* you bother to listen in the first place. The answer: you want to learn something.

Consider what happens when a boss walks into your office and praises you for excellent work. You're all ears. You're curious and aroused. You listen because you like the message and you want to hear more. You're not about to let your mind wander.

But when an employee raises an issue that's not particularly interesting or important to you, the last thing you want to do is drop whatever else you're thinking about so that you can give the speaker your undivided attention. You assume you have more to gain by not listening all that carefully, so you only make a halfhearted stab at going through the motions.

Here's a better way: commit to learning at least one fact or opinion from every employee you speak with today. Begin every conversation determined to get fresh ideas or insights from others. The more you listen to learn, the easier it'll become.

> **Teach Me, Teach Me**
>
> **Smart Managing** In order to listen better and learn from others, you must thirst for knowledge. To arouse your curiosity the next time you're feeling bored or restless, think to yourself, "Teach me, teach me" while you're listening to your employees. By repeating this phrase silently, you'll listen with more openness and absorb more information. Make this your "mantra" and you'll find yourself speaking less and listening more.

Curiosity begets more curiosity, and you'll experience a snowball effect as you start to capture a speaker's hopes, beliefs, and concerns with precision and accuracy. Once you begin to collect facts and opinions, you'll want to confirm them. That will lead you to ask follow-up questions and listen even more carefully to the answers.

There's another reason that it's a great idea to listen. When you listen to your employees, respect what they have to say, and take actions based on what they've told you, something very good starts to happen for you as a manager. That is that your employees will be more motivated to listen to you. In other words, when you listen, you teach the value of listening to others, and they will reciprocate. Of course, the same is true if you don't listen. When you don't pay attention to what your employees have to say, it becomes very difficult for them to pay much attention to you.

The Three Steps of Listening

Hearing and *listening* are entirely different.

Hearing refers to a physical act: your ears receive sound waves. As one of your senses, like seeing and touching, it doesn't require any real effort. That's why it's so easy to take for granted.

Listening, by contrast, tests your mental focus. You need to go beyond sensing incoming sounds so that you process what you hear. This unfolds in three steps: interpreting, assessing, and responding.

Interpreting

Once you hear something, you need to make sure you understand the message that the words convey. This involves a kind of quick mental translation in which you take what you hear and rephrase it in your own words.

A newly installed manager will often bring different vocabulary, experiences, and biases to a conversation with an employee. This can lead to crossed signals and mismatched messages. For example, if an entry-level worker tries to

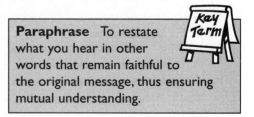

Paraphrase To restate what you hear in other words that remain faithful to the original message, thus ensuring mutual understanding.

warn you of a problem by saying, "I'm not so sure about that" when you make a suggestion, you can interpret that to mean:

- "I don't want to comply with your suggestion."
- "I doubt you're right."
- "I have more information to share with you if you pry it out of me."
- "I don't know as much about this as you do, so I defer to you."

You must clarify what the employee means before you respond. Each possible interpretation can determine a different direction for the conversation. Unless you follow up in a pleasant, nonthreatening tone, you may judge the employee's remark unfairly and draw the wrong conclusion.

A foolproof way to check your interpretation of what someone says is to repeat what you heard verbatim, but as a question. In the above example, you would respond, "You're not so sure about that?"

Speak in a neutral, curious manner; don't adopt an accusatory or angry voice. You'll find that the employee reveals more, thus enabling you to listen accurately and interpret the message as it was intended.

If you try to listen when you're angry or preoccupied, you may find it hard to interpret what you hear properly. That's all the more reason to repeat what others tell you as a question. Your moods and even your physiological state can affect whether speakers' words mean the same thing to you as they do to them.

Assessing

After you interpret a message, and only then, you judge it.

Poor or impatient listeners often skip the interpretation stage. They rush to evaluate what they hear, stamping messages with mental labels such as "right," "wrong," "smart," or "stupid." They instantly decide whether a speaker's comments are "worth it." They dismiss anything that strikes them negatively.

New managers are particularly susceptible to this "rush to judgment." They may read too much into what their employees tell them, and decide how they will use (or not use) the information they gather before they confirm they heard it correctly.

The best way to assess what you hear is to remain open-minded. Rather than box yourself in by thinking, "This makes no sense" or "This information doesn't help me at all," judge messages more charitably. Consider all sides of an issue. While you should still apply critical reasoning skills and listen attentively to every word, remain flexible and keep digging for

> **Bad Assessing = Bad News**
>
> **CAUTION!**
>
> Beware of evaluating messages based solely on whether you like or don't like what you hear. If you judge an employee's remarks harshly from the moment he or she starts talking, that will influence how you listen. Do not disregard information just because you're not comfortable with the nature or topic of the message. Overcome that obstacle. Accurately assess what your employee wants you to know. Evaluate it based on a dispassionate analysis of the facts, not a gut reaction or snap judgment.

information. Assessing works best when you're willing to reverse your judgments and reconsider firmly held assumptions or beliefs.

Responding

The first two stages of listening occur inside your head. You mentally translate a speaker's comment to gain understanding. Then you judge its value. Now it's time to respond, to let the world know that you're listening.

Your employees won't know if you've received their messages unless you respond. This is an external act, a way of signaling that you're listening.

Your response can be oral or visual. The most common way to respond is to say something, such as "I understand" or "Please go on." If you want to test the accuracy of your interpretation, you can restate what you hear as a question, as I mentioned above.

As a rule, it's smart not to respond by immediately presenting your point of view. Most employees want bosses who listen attentively and don't rush to interrupt. You'll earn their trust more quickly by responding with a follow-up question or a "prod statement" that invites them to talk some more.

You can also respond to a speaker with nonverbal cues. The most obvious examples are vigorous nods, beaming smiles, or looks of concern. Shaking your head in disgust or disagreement can indicate your displeasure, but it can also drive away employees who would otherwise come to you with their ideas or concerns. (And be sure that your expression clearly expresses your reaction. You may want to practice a little in front of a mirror, to see yourself as others see you. Your expressions may not be communicating as unambiguously as you assume they are.)

Prod statement A brief remark that prompts speakers to continue. You can elicit more information and gently prod them to elaborate with statements such as "This is interesting," "I see," or "Tell me more." Always follow a prod statement with silence. This gives the speaker permission to go on and shows that you're really intent on hearing more.

The best listening response is to maintain eye contact while showing interest in the speaker. Too much nodding and gesturing can actually distract an employee who's trying to tell you something.

"My manager starts nodding her head the moment I start talking," says a loan officer. "I start to talk faster, because I feel she's nodding because she wants me to get to my point quicker. It makes me uncomfortable."

When I met this person's boss, I thought that her frequent nodding was really a nervous tic. She would nod almost all the time, regardless of the speaker. She wasn't even aware of it. I put a small mirror near her desk in an unobtrusive position so that she could see for herself. After two days, she agreed she bobbed her head too much when she listened. Thanks to some relaxation exercises, she learned to keep still and respond more with eye contact than constant nodding.

We'll explore other aspects of listeners' body language in the pages that follow.

Fighting Off the Defensive Reflex

We're all only human and it's a very real world, so sometimes things bother us. Listening attentively is vital, but it's not always enough, especially when you don't like what you hear. The message can rub you the wrong way, and your irritation can block out what follows.

It's only natural to want to do something "to solve the problem" or "to right the wrong." And that can cause more problems and wrongs. The more you practice good listening skills, the sooner you'll learn to stay tuned to both positive and negative comments. Your hackles won't go up if somebody complains about something or criticizes you. You'll develop the discipline to assess the content of a speaker's remarks without instantly reacting to it.

New managers are particularly susceptible to the defensive reflex. When an employee complains or criticizes, it's a common trap for a novice supervisor to cut in with phrases such as "Hear me out a second" or "You've got it wrong."

> **Defensive reflex** The reflexive urge to defend yourself when you hear something that upsets you. Rather than pause, let the message sink in, and confirm understanding, you rush to contradict the speaker or justify your position. This defensive posture weakens your ability to listen and can change a conversation into a conflict.

There's a time and place for asserting your views or correcting a misperception. But first, you must demonstrate to your staffers that you've heard them. That takes patience. If they want to get something off their chest, then let them. Don't feel you must say a word. Your presence alone can show that you're willing to listen.

Before you defend yourself or mount a defense on behalf of others, such as your organization's senior management, check to make sure you can make an impact. Here's a quick test to tell if you're on safe ground to shift into defensive mode:

- You've let the speaker talk at will. You have not tried to rush, prod, or interrupt. You have not finished his or her sentences or shown impatience, such as by glancing at the clock.
- You've asked at least one question to indicate your interest in learning more.
- You've confirmed your understanding by paraphrasing the message accurately, to the satisfaction of the other person.

In your first few months as a new manager, you'll undoubtedly experience one of the most frustrating aspects of human communication: misunderstanding. You or your employee will struggle to make a point, maybe plead with the other, rephrase or repackage suggestions, and still it seems either you or the employee doesn't get it. You get frustrated and maybe end up getting angry with one another.

So what can you do?

First, remember you're a listening role model for your employees. Strive to prove to them that you appreciate what they're saying and how they're feeling. Rather than go through the motions with fake smiles and empty gestures, pay close attention and let them set the pace of the conversation. Get the employee to say—or at least think—"Yes, you (the manager) understand me." In other words, if you want to be understood, first make sure you go out of your way in any interaction to make sure you understand what your employees have to say.

"PAC" it in

Smart Managing   When you want to avoid the defensive reflex, remember the acronym "PAC." It stands for Patience-Ask-Confirm, and it corresponds to the three-prong test described above. As long as you've demonstrated patience, asked at least one question, and confirmed that you've understood the speaker accurately, then you're in a much better position to respond and state your case.

Even if the employee says things you don't agree with, don't discount what he or she is saying. That will turn on defense mechanisms that get in the way of understanding and cooperation. Remember this: listen for *understanding*, not *agreement*. Understanding doesn't mean agreement. You don't have to agree with what your employees are saying, and they don't have to agree with you.

Now, once you do have understanding, you can work on agreement. Disagreement is usually the result of people not having the same information or assumptions. By talking things through, respectfully listening to one another, and examining assumptions, you can usually end up with shared understanding *and* agreement.

How's Your Body Language?

You can be the best listener on earth, but if you start looking out the window just as your employee opens up to you, then you'll lose the connection. Use your eyes to show that you listen. Plant them on the speaker and nowhere else.

Think how you feel when you're trying to communicate with someone

⚠️ CAUTION!

Being Defensive Without Words

You can lapse into the defensive reflex without saying a thing. Examples of silent but deadly actions that can drive a wedge into your relationships with employees:
1. You shake your head vigorously while they're speaking as if to say, "No, no, no!"
2. You hold up your hand like a traffic cop, trying to get them to stop talking.
3. You roll your eyes, grimace in disgust, or otherwise appear like you want to put a sock in the speaker's mouth.

who appears distracted. You're trying to make an important point, and you begin to feel like the other person is disinterested and detached. You notice these trouble signs:

- **A wandering eye.** Rather than look at you most of the time, the listener's eyes dart about nervously. He or she may look away to see who's walking by or to check messages that pop up on the computer screen.

- **A physical preoccupation.** Rather than listen calmly, others are constantly scratching their necks or arms, rubbing their eyes, running their hand through their hair, crossing and uncrossing their legs, or similar actions.
- **Yawning.** If someone looks tired, you've got to prune away fluff and cut straight to the crux of your message. You can just sense that the more you talk, the less good it does.

Remember how irritated you feel when you want to make yourself heard and the other person just doesn't seem to be there with you. That should motivate you to listen more intently and send the right signals that you're ready, willing, and able to soak it all in. (It doesn't matter if you actually listen better when you're gazing out the window or staring at the ceiling. This is about communicating your interest.)

As you listen, lean slightly toward the speaker if you're more than a few feet away. This conveys your desire to hear every word. This works especially well if you run into an employee in a noisy hallway or on the factory floor and you start chatting.

Show that you actually *want* to listen.

Body Language—Three Tips

TRICKS OF THE TRADE I advised a jittery executive how to improve his body language so that his employees didn't feel neglected when they spoke with him. He was concerned after years of getting feedback that he was "easily distracted" and had a "short attention span." I observed his behavior and suggested three ways to improve it:

- **Face the speaker.** He tended to turn slightly to his side when listening. As a result, employees assumed he was somehow objecting to their comments, bored, or standoffish.
- **Look into eyeballs.** He thought he gave great eye contact. But when I chatted with him, he kept looking at my forehead, as if I had some pimple that fascinated him. I coached him to lower his gaze slightly so that it was eye to eye.
- **Keep your hands free.** He always liked to play with his pen. When others spoke, he would absentmindedly flip it, click it, and sometimes roll it back and forth across his desk.

Manager's Checklist for Chapter 4

❏ Before you respond, count silently to three. This prevents you from interrupting, which allows the speaker to elaborate or reveal more information.

❏ Train yourself to listen better by striving to learn at least one fact or opinion from every conversation.

❏ Interpret, assess, and respond to what you hear patiently and systematically. Don't jump right to the third step and respond prematurely.

❏ Apply the "PAC" method to avoid instantly defending yourself when you hear criticism: *p*atiently listen, *a*sk at least one question, and *c*onfirm that you've heard the speaker accurately.

❏ Listen for *understanding*, not *agreement*. Make room for differences in opinion or outlook.

❏ Identify yourself with a speaker's interests, and maintain friendly eye contact so that your body language signals that you want to listen.

Speak Like a Leader

After two months as a manager, Barbara met with her friend Sally to get some feedback on her performance as a boss. Even though the two women started as aides in the same department, Sally now reported to Barbara.

"Barbara, you talk differently now than you did before you were a manager," Sally said. "You sound a bit stiff, and your natural warmth doesn't come across like it used to. It's like you take everything you say so seriously."

That in a nutshell is the biggest trap new managers face: they try to speak the way they think "a boss should speak." That may mean adopting a deeper voice, giving unsolicited opinions, and issuing commands to show their authority.

Yet the best way to radiate power is to express it naturally. There's no one "right" speaking style. You don't have to give stirring speeches or crack funny jokes on cue. The more genuine you come across, the more you can make yourself clear and generate buy-in from your staff.

A Voice That Roars

For the first few days as a new manager, people will judge you like you've never been judged before. Like students checking out a new teacher, your employees will watch your every move and draw quick conclusions about your poise and leadership. You're probably thinking, "In that case, I better dress just right, learn everyone's name, and not say anything stupid."

Fair enough. Yet there's something that you may take for granted but that is more powerful than any other single factor in influencing how your employees perceive you—your voice. This is a tool that almost always gets overlooked by managers who're trying to sharpen their communication skills.

A bad voice can misrepresent you. It can alienate your staff, undermine your credibility, and betray your true feelings. It can even cause you physical pain if you don't treat it properly.

This doesn't mean you need to consult with a speech coach on pitch, tone, volume, tempo, and breath control. While each of these elements can help you speak dynamically, your primary goal as a new manager is simply to make your voice work *for* you, not *against* you.

Your Own Worst Enemy?

Ruth and Scott were both appointed to manage the help desk at a large bank and oversee the work of computer technicians. I was training them on skills they'd need as new managers, when we got around to discussing the need for clear, commanding communication.

"I'm already in trouble," Ruth said. "Next week, Scott and I are going to address our employees. Scott goes first, and he's got this deep, powerful voice. Then I'll get up there and people will strain to hear me. I'll sound really weak."

I told Ruth the good news: her voice could actually prove a tremendous asset—not a liability. Her clear enunciation and self-assured pacing would draw listeners in, not drive them away.

"You don't have to try to sound like Scott," I said. "It's a fact that men and women sound different. The key is to make yourself understood and to use your voice to reinforce your message."

You're not necessarily the best judge of your voice. I've heard nervous managers confess that they feared their first day in a new job because they would sound too mousy, too mean, too scared, too dull, too strict, or too bossy. I've heard them insist they had a terrible accent, a natural whisper, a chronically hoarse throat, or an embarrassing lisp.

Yet from the hundreds of managers I've advised, only about 1% were right to worry about their voice. These few individuals *did* have a problem that needed fixing. The others all just convinced themselves they sounded far worse than they actually did.

Get a Reality Check

On a sheet of paper, create four columns with the following headings: volume, tempo, inflection, clarity. Photocopy this sheet and give a copy to three trusted friends or colleagues. Now rate your voice on a 1-to-10 scale (with 10 the best) in each of these categories. Ask your three associates to do the same, encouraging them to be completely honest. Leave room on the page for them to explain their ratings or include additional feedback on your voice. Review their "score sheets" and compare them with your own. Evaluate to what extent you perceive your voice as others do.

So, you may sound better than you fear, but don't get complacent: you can still improve. First, practice your inflection. Emphasize only those words that you want to highlight. Beware of ending declarative sentences with an upward inflection; this can lead your staffers to think you're unsure of what you're saying and/or of yourself. When you ask a question, make sure to inflect on the last word; this indicates you're now going to keep quiet and await an answer. (And make sure that you stop there.)

Also pay attention to how you project your voice, especially when you're addressing a group. Always begin talking to the individual seated farthest from you. This ensures that you'll be speaking loudly enough for everyone else to hear. Then watch for facial expressions or shifts in posture that indicate that some people may be having problems hearing you.

Remember to pause frequently so that you don't string words together. Fast talkers often get into trouble by trying to

pack too much into too little time. If you're explaining something or repeating lots of information, don't assume just
because it's familiar to you that it'll sound equally familiar to
your employees.

Package Your Points

As the boss, what you say goes. But if you bark too many
orders without trying to explain your thinking or educate your
staff, then you risk turning into a tyrant.

When you speak to employees, your goal should be to
express your points in a way that makes it easy for them to
understand you. If you hop from topic to topic in a disorderly
fashion, you can leave a trail of confusion and noncompliance
in your wake.

To present your points in an easy-to-understand manner,
think before you speak. Sift through what you want to say and
select only the most relevant, timely comments. That way, you
avoid overloading your employees with too many details and
you also help ensure that you say what you need to say.

Many new managers
assume they know how to
make themselves clear.
They take communication
for granted. Rather than
pause to plan what they
want to say, they plunge
right in and eventually get
around to the main point—
babbling the whole time.
They wing it and force their
employees to struggle to
figure out what's been said.

There's a better way. It
involves thinking in threes,
or breaking down your
remarks into three distinct

It's Not Too Late

The French have an
expression that refers to
all the clever and insightful things you
think to say only after you part company with someone: *esprit d'escalier*—
which translates as "spirit of the stair-
way," which is often where such
thoughts come to us. There's nothing
more frustrating than realizing you
forgot to warn or advise an employee
about a key issue, and then wishing
you could replay the conversation and
get it right. By mapping out what you
want to say ahead of time, you can
avoid the regret that comes with
lamenting the points that went unsaid.

parts. You'll find that your staff can readily grasp ideas that come grouped in three. You might say, "There are three steps to this process," "I have three reasons for asking you to do this," or "Let's evaluate this idea on three different levels." By using such "pointer" phrases, you let your listeners know what's coming: you're about to deliver a trio of points.

Clustering your remarks in threes works especially well when you want to persuade your employees to buy into your ideas. They'll find it harder to argue or rebut your points if you deliver three appropriate forms of support. Providing only one or two facts or assertions to back up your position may not prove too convincing, but when you add a third piece of evidence you can shut down potential resistance. This can be especially effective if you tick the points off on your fingers as you make them.

When Phil Marineau took over as Pepsi's new North American beverage chief in 1998, he clearly stated that raising Pepsi-Cola's sales was his No. 1 priority. He emphasized his "three R's" strategy—to *reexamine, rethink,* and *revitalize* the Pepsi trademark. Similarly, when Robert Nakasone took over as CEO of Toys 'R' Us in 1998, he announced that his toy stores would be converted using what he called the "C-3" format—to make them *cost-effective, customer-driven,* and *concept-oriented* for the future.

You can speak with more authority by harnessing the power of three. If you talk too much and list too many reasons why

Make Your Case Airtight

When Ron, a new manager, tried to persuade his 10 employees to fill out activity reports, they balked and gave excuses. Then he said, "There are three reasons why I'd like you to complete these reports. One, you'll find they help you get more done in less time, thus allowing you to get home at a reasonable hour. Two, you'll learn what obstacles keep you from spending more time on your favorite projects. And three, you'll qualify for incentive raises, because I intend to use these reports as one way to evaluate you."

you think you're right, you'll tax the patience of your staff. They will tune out and dismiss you as a lecturing blowhard. On the other hand, if you fail to give three solid points, they may remain skeptical, drill holes in your argument, or perhaps just walk away without committing to your position.

Most new managers find it easy to think in threes. The hard part is stopping once they're on a roll! You need to keep quiet after you deliver your trio of points. If you ramble or repeat yourself, then you'll lose your employees' attention.

Here are some ways to present your package of points in threes:

- Let's study this in three different ways.
- Let's consider the three strongest reasons to go ahead with this.
- There are three factors driving this decision.
- There's a three-prong test we can apply to this problem.
- The three most important things to remember are ...

The three tactic also works effectively in other situations, not just when you're presenting three points or three methods or three factors. Here are two examples.

When instructing or coaching your employees, a handy way to communicate with them is to speak in terms of *problem-cause-solution*. Begin by saying, "We need to confront this problem, find its cause, and propose solutions." Then proceed to walk them through each of the three stages, posing questions and giving guidance as needed.

A similar way to package your ideas in threes is to discuss *facts-analysis-recommendation*. Introduce your employees to the key facts that they must absorb in order to make headway. Then prod them to analyze the significance of the facts. Your goal is to help them answer the questions, "What does all this mean?" and "What are the consequences?" Wrap up by inviting them to make suggestions or formal recommendations that flow from their analysis.

Prune Away Fluff

Many new managers undergo a rite of passage that I call the "nervous Nellie" phase. They are afraid to assert their authority or speak their mind. Until they get accustomed to their role, they're riddled with doubt or uncertainty whenever they answer their staff's questions or try to teach or discipline them. It's not a pretty sight.

In keeping with the spirit of the previous section, here are three ways to tell if you're a "nervous Nellie":

1. **You overdose on qualifiers.** Rookie managers often hesitate to commit to even the most simple statements. Instead of declaring, "This old phone system has to go," they say, "Maybe this old phone system should be replaced." They qualify their remarks with words such as "perhaps," "maybe," and "generally." While that's fine if you're a lawyer who must choose every word with extreme precision and then qualify it for extra safety, that "soft touch" can weaken your stature if you're a new manager struggling to prove yourself to your staff.

2. **You repeat yourself.** If you're anxious, you may rehash the same point so much that your employees get tired of nodding their heads. If you assume that you need to make yourself abundantly clear, then you may insist on repeating or rephrasing basic instructions or observations ad nauseam. Strategic repetition enforces, but wandering around through the same points again and again just undermines the strength of your words.

3. **You ramble.** One reason to think in threes is it helps you stay on track. If you plunge right in and start lecturing or pontificating to your staff, you may wind up rambling aimlessly. You'll jump from topic to topic randomly, leaving your listeners bewildered. They won't retain what you say, regardless of how many valid points you make, because it will be too hard for them to separate the wheat from the chaff.

And Now the News ...

Barry took over a transaction-processing unit at a bank. At first, he would pummel his staff into submission with his long-winded comments. They would avoid encounters for fear of hearing him babble on and on. When Barry told me he used to work as a night copy editor for his local newspaper and write headlines such as "Cubs beat Mets" and "President signs tax bill," I seized on that to coach him to improve as a manager. I said, "Talk to your staff the way you wrote headlines: subject, verb, object. Then stop talking and let them respond."

Accept that you'll be nervous in your first days or weeks as a new manager. Like a jittery public speaker, however, you must ensure that your butterflies fly in formation. That means transforming your anxiety into positive energy.

As a manager, you need to communicate with clarity and force. Less is more. By pruning away fluff and sticking to the core message, you make it easier for your employees to understand you. Better yet, you leave more time for them to respond. As Lyndon Johnson said, "You can't learn nothin' if you're talkin'."

To prevent your anxiety from turning you into a motor mouth, treat your words as a precious resource. Don't feel compelled to repeat yourself or add examples or anecdotes. After you complete a sentence, pause and give everyone a chance to reflect. Let a few seconds pass and see if anyone jumps in. Beware of running on like a steamroller that just keeps flattening everything in its path.

Don't feel a need to exaggerate or inflate the importance of what you're saying. Keep your comments short and sweet; then engage your employees in a true give-and-take interaction. This enables you to win their respect while training them to listen attentively to your every word. They won't tune out if they know you're not likely to repeat yourself.

If you try too hard to sound the way you think a manager should sound, you risk losing credibility. Consider how two *Washington Post* reporters described the speaking style of

House Speaker Newt Gingrich in 1995: "He spoke in sweeping sentences bursting with adjectives and adverbs that rendered his words oversized and absolute. Enormous. Classic. Grotesque. Tremendous. Totally. Frankly. Unequivocally. Extraordinarily. Explicitly."

> **The 80/20 Principle**
> **Smart Managing** To avoid wasting words, strive to limit your speaking to 20% of the time and listen to your staffers the remaining 80% of the conversation. This applies primarily when you're trying to persuade, although it's a useful benchmark for most types of everyday encounters. Exception: When you want to explain a complex procedure or inform your staff of many new developments, then you may need to speak more than one-fifth of the time.

Loading your speech with words such as "frankly" and "extraordinarily" weakens it by giving it weight without substance. That style may be appropriate for a demagogue, but not for a manager. You can use such words occasionally, but for emphasis. Use them all the time and you sound pretentious, and they lose meaning.

Your staff doesn't need to hear you carry on. Whether you're nervous or self-centered, your best bet is to cut the fat from your remarks and be more effective with just muscle.

Ask the Right Questions Right

There's an art to posing questions. By choosing the proper phrasing and speaking in a genuinely curious, inquisitive tone, you can help employees discover lessons for themselves—and you may learn a lot yourself.

New managers often hesitate to ask questions under the mistaken impression that they're supposed to have all the answers. They may assume that admitting they don't know something is akin to showing a weakness.

"I figured when I became a manager that I would tell people what to do and, if necessary, how to do it," admitted a marketing manager after a year in the job. "It took me a while to realize that my people hated being told what to do. They want me to help them, but not to strip away their dignity and their ability to think for themselves."

When you ask questions, you show your employees that you respect their ideas and opinions. You're letting them know that you're their manager, not the font of all wisdom. You want to learn from them and you're willing to invest the time to hear what they have to say.

Better yet, you enhance your stature as a leader worth listening to. As a result of all your questions, you can then render judgments or issue orders that the troops will more readily respect. You can preface your conclusions by saying, "Thanks to all of your input..." or "You've all taken a lot of time helping me understand this, and I'm grateful. Now I've decided ...."

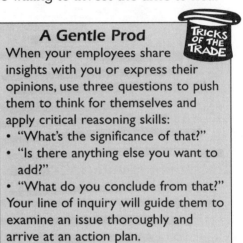

A Gentle Prod

When your employees share insights with you or express their opinions, use three questions to push them to think for themselves and apply critical reasoning skills:

• "What's the significance of that?"
• "Is there anything else you want to add?"
• "What do you conclude from that?"

Your line of inquiry will guide them to examine an issue thoroughly and arrive at an action plan.

Like any communication skill, questioning can backfire if misused. If you reel off a series of accusatory or loaded questions, such as "You didn't do what I asked, did you?" "What are you not telling me?" or "Did it occur to you that there's more to it than that?" you invite scorn. Interrogate employees and you will alienate them. Posing questions dripping with dismay or disapproval will stir their resentment.

Consider the negativity behind the question, "Why didn't you tell me that would take so long?" Most employees will instantly defend themselves; they'll explain all that went wrong (and possibly how *you* contributed to the mess) to avoid the blame. Meanwhile, you've lost a chance to build rapport. A less hostile question—such as "How did you approach this project?" or "What steps did you take?"—can help you understand why something took "so long" while still maintaining a pleasant, nonthreatening dialogue with your

CAUTION!

I Care ... Really!

Don't use questions because you think you should show interest even when you don't really care. If you aren't curious about the answer, then just keep quiet. An employee can sense when you're just going through the motions without caring. Your questions will lose their meaning, and you'll appear distracted. Result: you do more damage than if you never asked the question at all.

employee. (Just be careful with your tone, which can put an edge on the most carefully chosen words.)

Always maintain eye contact with your employee when you ask a question. Don't fidget, read, or eat. If you try to do two things at once, you give the impression that you're not paying full attention to their answer.

A little earlier, we discussed the importance of pruning away fluff so that you don't talk too much. Same goes when you question others. Keep your inquiries to one sentence. Never lace a ques-

Key Term

Drowning question A question that drowns the listener in verbiage. Rather than pose a simple, one-sentence question, you toss in lots of extra questions, side comments, and even answers to your own questions. The result: a confused employee who's unsure where to begin when you finally finish up.

tion with lots of editorial comments or asides that test the patience of your employees. Come right out and ask what you want to know—and then stop talking!

Whenever you ask a question, stop immediately afterward. Close your mouth and await a response. If there's a few

seconds of silence, don't fret. Some employees need a little extra time to think before they talk. You should allow it—even expect it. (For one thing, it shows that they weren't thinking of what to say while you were talking!) Never jump in to repeat or rephrase the question, unless about seven seconds pass and you're unsure whether the person heard you. Seven seconds will seem like an eternity, but it's enough time for almost anyone to gather their thoughts and at least take a stab at giving you an answer. (This holds true whether you're on the phone or speaking in person.)

Make Your Words Sink In

When Tracy, the newly appointed leader of a computer training unit, instructed her employee to learn a new software program, she kept saying, "Don't do that" or "That won't work." Then she would demonstrate the "right" way to proceed.

As you might expect, Tracy's employee didn't feel great about the training session. After a few minutes, it felt like all Tracy could say was "No, you're wrong." Instead, Tracy should have let her trainee experiment with the program while playing a less hands-on role. If her employee tried to bypass certain commands, for instance, Tracy could have said, "When I've done that, it erased my file. Let's see if that happens to you." This helps both parties learn together, and Tracy doesn't make her subordinate feel like an order-taker.

To speak like a leader, you need to avoid making remarks that threaten or demean others. Examples of poor communication styles include bluntly contradicting someone, habitually volunteering your opinion, and rashly judging others. New managers may not realize just how often they make one of these mistakes.

When you disagree with an employee, say so. But speak diplomatically. Use phrases such as "I under-

> **Overdosing on "I"**
>
> Inexperienced managers tend to use "I" too much, especially when they want to sound more formal or official. Avoid saying, "I felt he lacked product knowledge" or "I'm not pleased with that supplier because he never delivers on time." Strengthen your comments by saying just "He lacked product knowledge" or "That supplier never delivers on time." Chop away the "I" so that the subject of the sentence is who you're talking about. However, if you're really offering an opinion, it's OK to use "I" to indicate that.

stand what you're saying, and I have to disagree" or "That's one way to look at it, although my experience leads me to a different conclusion." Don't feel a need to elaborate or justify your position in detail. *Instead, stop and let the employee respond.* Launch a

From What You've Told Me ...

Will needed to prod one of his least committed employees to work harder. He had tried before, but the employee ultimately gave the same half-hearted effort. This time, Will said, "You told me something the other day that stayed with me. You said that you're perfectly happy to be left alone, that you don't need much management. I'm happy to oblige, but you'll make it easier for me to leave you alone if you meet certain performance standards." By acknowledging his employee's preferences and proving how well he had listened and retained what he was told, Will convinced this individual to improve.

friendly conversation, remain attentive, and treat what you hear seriously. Never prejudge or dismiss outright what a staffer says. You may even find that the person knows more than you about a subject or activity, and his or her input may change your mind.

To maximize the odds that your team retains what you're about to say, tie it to something they've already said. Play back the same words they've used as a way to show that you listened and understood and then to relate what you're saying to their interests or concerns. If you want them to buy into yet another procedural change, begin by saying, "You've told me many times that you want ..." or "Remember at last week's meeting when you asked me ...." After you remind them of their past comments, connect your new message so that it fits right into the context of their wishes or requests.

To ensure that your words sink in, never rush to give commands and then walk away. Employees resent a manager who barks orders at a rapid pace, only to cut the conversation short at a moment's notice. You'll leave your listeners bewildered and probably annoyed.

Try to invest a few minutes in confirming that your staff understood your comments. Solicit their feedback with questions such as "Does this make sense?" or "Is there anything else you think we should consider?"

If you're on the phone, don't hang up until you get at least some acknowledgment that the other party heard you. Ideally, this happens when your employee summarizes your remarks or reviews what actions need to occur. To avoid misunderstandings, check that you made yourself clear by saying, "Tell me how you'll proceed from here."

By leaving time for others to respond, you can create a more comfortable give-and-take in which employees demonstrate that they paid attention to you. Rather than guess that your words sunk in, you'll know beyond any doubt that message you sent reached its destination intact.

Manager's Checklist for Chapter 5

❏ Pause frequently to avoid stringing words together. Project your voice clearly, especially when you're addressing a group.

❏ Think in threes. Prepare a trio of points that you want to make so that you give employees enough support to substantiate your views—without going overboard and talking too much.

❏ Avoid qualifiers that weaken your message or needlessly reveal your doubts.

❏ When you're trying to persuade an employee, limit your speaking to 20% of the time and listen during the remaining 80% of the conversation. This ensures you'll treat your words as a precious resource.

❏ Avoid blatantly contradicting employees; instead, propose "another way of looking at it."

❏ To increase the odds that your staffers understand and retain what you say, tie your messages to what they've told you before.

The Art of
Motivation

When a manager complains to me, "I wish I could motivate Gus," here's what he really means: I wish I could get Gus to do his job better.

The whole point of trying to help your employees feel motivated is to help them become more productive as well as happy about their work and thus not want to move on to another job. The stronger their commitment to superior performance, the easier it becomes to motivate them. It's like preaching to the choir. Apathetic individuals probably won't respond to your motivational management because they just don't *want* to do well; they're content to give you a minimal effort and see no reason to push any harder.

New managers often assume that they're great motivators if they communicate enthusiastically and see changes in employees' behavior. But getting workers to pump their fists or act like cheerleaders won't matter much if they're not competent or reliable. They need to feel a desire to do better, to learn more, to develop their skills. That's why true motivation does more than modify an individual's behavior: it lifts the level of performance and produces a more valuable, committed employee.

Before we look at specific techniques, here are three basic rules of effective motivation:

1. Never ask others to do anything you wouldn't do yourself.
2. Provide your employees with feedback. Don't wait for periodic performance reviews.
3. Encourage them to talk with you about the good *and* bad aspects of their job. If they complain on occasion, don't label them as malcontents and dismiss their comments. Listen and understand what bothers them before you judge.

Press the Right Buttons

Some medical schools now require their students to spend time as patients in a hospital. They're assigned a certain disease, a role to play. The hospital doesn't know they're really students. The experience of getting poked, probed, and pushed from room to room changes their outlook, and these students often claim to learn more from this exercise than from any textbook.

You're more fortunate than those med students, because not too long ago you were one of those employees or at least an employee in a similar situation, so you know how it feels. You understand the pressures they face and the environment within which they operate. Before you took on the role of manager, you knew what matters most to the employees. You knew how they make decisions, handle adversity, and derive satisfaction from their work. And that should take the guesswork out of motivating them.

Perhaps you can identify with some of the anxieties and irritations that your current staff feels. Cling to these memories and keep them fresh. Those feelings and those experiences can be invaluable as you develop skills that will help employees feel motivated to perform well.

Also realize that there's no single secret to the way you interact with employees to increase their motivation on the job. Everyone's different, so you'll need to tailor your approach for each employee.

Edward J. Feeney, a management consultant, recalls a firm that hired an independently wealthy woman as a phone reservation agent. The company soon wanted to fire her for poor performance, but first her managers tried to learn what motivated her. They found she loved to suggest ideas and improvements, so they proposed an unusual scheme: whenever she attained her target for making reservations, she earned 15 minutes with the manager to discuss her ideas. This incentive made her an excellent agent.

Reach Out with Empathy

Motivation begins with empathy. When you can step into another person's shoes and appreciate their attitudes and concerns, you can then identify their priorities, values, and beliefs. Based on this awareness, you can isolate the hot-button issues that they care about most. This in turn enables you to appeal to each of your employees personally. Your attempt to spur employee motivation begins with understanding each employee, and it builds on that one-to-one relationship.

The best way to empathize is to clear away all your biases and assumptions when you relate to others. Ask yourself, "If I were [employee], what would matter most to me?" The more often you stop and chat with this person and listen attentively to his or her comments, the sooner you'll answer your question. Note what topics each employee raises with you; a sure way to uncover someone's hot buttons is to pay attention to their gripes, jokes, and requests.

TRICKS OF THE TRADE

Tell Me More

To instill a feeling of motivation in someone, get to know the person and empathize. Ask frequent questions: "Are you happy with your progress?" "Are you pleased with your office?" "Do you enjoy your work?" "Is there enough challenge for you?" Don't settle for neutral or noncommittal answers. Prod them to reveal more. After about a dozen of these conversations, you'll start to notice recurring subjects that each employee tends to raise, ranging from concern over lack of teamwork to disappointment with the company's policies and procedures. This tells you what employees care about most. Use this information to interact more effectively with them, to keep them feeling good about their jobs and motivated to perform well.

Motivation is not a spectator sport. You can't empathize with people from afar, and you can't delegate this task to others. There's no way to step into someone else's shoes unless you invest time in getting to know them. If you drop in on an employee once every few months, say "Great job!" then rush off in a flash, and assume you've worked some kind of motivational magic, guess again. Such a hurried display can actually do more harm than good, because it makes people feel unimportant, just another body on your rounds.

The only way to help people feel motivated is eyeball-to-eyeball. You must devote time to talk with people. By regularly interacting with them in a positive way, you will build the kind of camaraderie that leads to a more energized work force.

"Above all else, good leaders are open," said Jack Welch, General Electric's longtime CEO, in an interview with *Harvard Business Review*. "They go up, down, and around their organization to reach people. They make a religion out of being accessible." Since Welch became CEO, G.E. has been one of the most successful companies in the world, earning Welch *Fortune* magazine's recognition as CEO of the century.

Isolate the Need

If you want to press the right buttons, you must know what to look for. All employees are different, but you can still generalize about what motivates them.

Prior to the rash of downsizings in the late 1980s, many employees expected safety and security. If you could give them a steady income, a relatively stable, predictable work environment, and a generous pension plan, they were happy. Managers didn't need to worry as much about employee motivation, because maintaining their careers was enough to keep them feeling motivated to perform.

Today's workers are altogether tougher and more complex. Few employees expect a job to insulate them from the harsh elements and threats of the unknown; issues of safety and security rarely matter as much in this fluid, rapidly changing economy.

Instead, most people are motivated by one of these six needs: attainment, power, belonging, independence, respect, and equity.

In your first few months as a manager, you may have trouble determining which one of these six hot buttons is most important to each of your subordinates. Here's how you can tell:

Attainment. Some employees love the act of achieving something. They want to sharpen their skills to reach greater heights, and they're generally pleased if you can give them assignments that force them to stretch a bit and overcome considerable challenges. You can spot these employees by their goal-driven determination and their willingness to ignore office politics in favor of sinking their teeth into a project that tests their talents and harnesses their skills. Motivate them by constantly introducing new tasks that build on each other. Allow them to work toward both short- and long-term goals, thus creating a record of achievement and growth.

Power. Some individuals thrive on exerting influence and control. They like the spotlight and the feeling of importance that comes from calling the shots. These employees usually try to hog center stage at meetings and state bold, controversial opinions. They also may attract attention with their high-visibility interest in leadership positions, such as volunteering to serve as team spokesperson. This type of individual may buttonhole the chief executive officer at a party, express delight when experiencing corporate perks (such as visiting the executive suite or going out to lunch with bigwigs), and curry favor with high-level consultants and other outsiders who radiate power and authority. Treat these employees like in-house experts and frequently ask them for advice. This will instantly plug into what makes them feel motivated because they'll savor the chance to offer their opinions and see that you take them seriously.

Belonging. Employees who want to feel a sense of comradeship are among the easiest to make feel motivated: just leave them alone to build rapport with their coworkers. Make sure they have plenty of chances to get to know their colleagues in informal settings, such as company picnics and other outings that occur outside of the normal work day. Because these individuals find the social aspects of their job the most meaningful, you can motivate them by making them feel like they're part of a larger group. For example, arrange meetings where they can collaborate and share ideas, rather than sit and listen to lectures or formal presentations. Satisfy their need for affiliation and they'll give you a solid effort.

Independence. Some employees seek autonomy above all else. They want the freedom to experiment with their job assignments and function at least somewhat independently. If you micromanage their every move, you'll deaden their desire to go the extra mile. You'll know you're managing independent workers if you find that they chafe whenever you enact new policies or procedures. They will reject new rules and rebel against bossy supervisors. The best way to connect with what motivates these freedom-seekers is to give them overriding goals and let them find the best way to produce results. Without showing favoritism, try giving them the flexibility to set their own hours, make unhindered choices, and decide what steps they want to take to get the job done.

Respect. Like comedian Rodney Dangerfield, some employees simply want a little respect. These individuals may storm out of a room if they feel ignored or "dissed." They also may follow rules of office etiquette to the extreme, dressing conservatively in well-pressed clothes and cultivating an almost military bearing. If you listen to them, they'll feel more motivated. Nod and give them full eye contact when they talk. Avoid checking your watch or doing paperwork while they're speaking to you. Don't interrupt them or shake your head in disagreement as soon as they open their mouth. Also lavish them with recognition and feedback on their performance, especially praise. While you should treat all employees with respect, these behaviors are particularly important when you're trying to fulfill an employee's need for esteem.

Equity. While everyone likes to work for a fair, unbiased boss, some employees see the world almost exclusively through the eyes of just versus unjust. They may compare how you manage your staff's work schedules, job titles, scope of responsibilities, pay, and benefits to ensure there are no hints of inequities. They take it upon themselves to police your authority. They will not hesitate to tell you if they think something's unfair, and they'll eagerly point out inconsistencies in your management style and decision-making. You can plug into what motivates these employees by thinking like an employment lawyer: give them objective evidence to prove that you're a fair, equitable boss. For example, distribute industry-wide salary surveys to show these employees how you arrived at pay scales and explain how compensation relates to job grade or job description. Tell them you will not tolerate any hint of bias or impropriety. Encourage them to let you know if they perceive any evidence of inequity so that you have a chance to investigate and, if necessary, correct it.

Moving Beyond Money

Many new managers assume making employees feel motivated is a breeze. They figure as long as they can throw money at employees they'll perform like trained seals.

While cash certainly counts for most of us, it's overrated as a motivational tool. It's the lifeblood of business, but it doesn't necessarily drive every employee to excel or even to care.

"I've learned you motivate people by treating them like you want to be treated," Richard Jenrette told me. Jenrette, the co-founder of the Wall Street firm Donaldson Lufkin & Jenrette, is also the retired chairman and CEO of the Equitable Companies, an insurance firm. "Money alone won't do it. Let me give you an example. I just met with a talented guy who got a $30 million bonus from a big Wall Street brokerage firm. But then he quit. Why? Because no one called him to congratulate him. A check just showed up with no note, nothing. 'I figured they didn't care,' he said. He lost the motivation to work there because he felt no one noticed him."

Same goes if you seek to extract extra time and effort from your already overworked team. Don't dangle cash rewards and conclude that's all the motivation they'll need. Instead, appeal to their sense of pride and responsibility for a job well done.

Give employees ways to exert control or influence over their work. Most people have a psychological need to shape their daily lives, rather than react helplessly as crises pelt them from all sides. You'll not only motivate your staff but also cut their stress level by respecting their ability to call at least some of the shots.

Another strategy to plug into employee motivation without money is to show how you intend to track your employees' work product. As seasoned managers often like to say, "What you measure is what you get." For instance, if you want to rally your troops to double-check their work before turning it in, say, "I'll be tracking your reports and recognizing those employees who do error-free work." Then follow through and publicly praise those individuals who consistently produce work without mistakes.

Motivate with Responsibility

In a survey of 1,500 managerial, technical, and professional workers by Response Analysis in Princeton, NJ, the reason most often cited for employees who put in voluntary effort was having responsibility for results. Other factors such as money ranked lower. Conclusion: let your employees make decisions and produce results on their own and they'll be more motivated to volunteer and go beyond the call of duty.

"As a manager, what you *do* is two times as important as what you *say* when you want to connect with what motivates your employees," said Don Harrison, president of Implementation Management Associates, a consulting firm in Brighton, CO. "And what you *reinforce* is three times as important as what you say. Managers underestimate the amount of scrutiny they're under by their employees, so they need to constantly reinforce what they want to send a clear message to their employees."

Strive to tie an individual's hard work to a meaningful, concrete result. If you want your team to feel motivated to enact a new procedure, tell them that their compliance will help the company reduce its paper usage by 7% and cut its administrative expenses by 10% over the next year. The fact that you and they know they can make a difference in the bottom line can serve as sufficient motivation in itself. Help your staff equate their effort with something real, as opposed to saying, "Do this and you'll be a hero."

Recognition is free. Salute the genuinely fine work of your employees, and you're assured of motivating them. Express praise in public and private. Never fear you'll overdo it, as long as you can honestly express admiration or gratitude. Seldom can money make a worker feel as elated as a manager who takes the time to smile and say, "Your contribution to this project was absolutely invaluable" or "You set such a great example of what I'm looking for here. Great job!"

Let's say you get to know your employees and you conclude that they're eager to advance in your organization. Ambitious people may want more than your recognition. Introduce them to upper management, and you might really be plugging into what motivates them. Gather a few of your firm's senior executives to mingle with your team at an informal meeting. Or invite to lunch a few of the staffers you want to motivate and bring along *your* boss to join you. If you can't line up any bigwigs to spend time with your employees, then establish cross-departmental teams and select your star employees to participate. This helps them fulfill their need for advancement and thus enhances their motivation to perform.

A great motivational technique is to treat employees' ideas seriously and respond promptly to their sensible proposals and valid complaints. Whether you set up a formal "suggestion box" or simply keep an open-door policy and hear them out, do not ignore their input. The very act of following up quickly will help them feel motivated to try harder and feel better about you and the whole organization.

> ## Playing the Fixer
>
> Roger took over as manager of the purchasing unit. On his first day, an employee approached him and said, "It's too noisy in here. We can't concentrate." Then the employee gave him a survey by the American Society of Interior Designers that said 70% of 1,000 respondents felt their productivity would increase if their offices were quieter. Roger promised to do something, and he did. Two days later, he told the employee, "I followed up on that study and found 81% of executives surveyed said they were unconcerned about office noise! Thanks to you, I'm not going to be one of them. Let's figure out a solution together." Roger thus displayed masterful motivational skill.

Knowledge: The Ultimate Motivator

While there's no foolproof method that will instantly transform every one of your staffers into hard-charging superstars, you can bet that they will almost all respond well to the gift of knowledge. Give people the chance to learn and grow both personally and professionally, and they will invest more of themselves in the job.

Dangle training and other learning opportunities as rewards for fine work. Select your most diligent or outstanding employees to attend outside seminars and conferences where they can expand their network, pick up new skills, and return to work with fresh perspectives. Sit down for 30 minutes with a high-potential newcomer and show how to master a tough task, leaving time for a demonstration. Make your office a place where everyone shares insights freely and collaborates to find better ways to work.

While we've already warned you that money isn't necessarily the only or best way to plug into what motivates employees (or you, for that matter), helping employees learn how the organization makes it can produce a big payoff. The more you can demystify the innards of your business and help your workers track the cash flow throughout your company, the more they'll tie their job and how they add value to the firm's larger, bottom-line performance. In fact, 59% of employees in an Ernst & Young survey said the best way to motivate them is for their managers

Welcome to the Roundtable

Consider creating a new tradition at your company called a "Roundtable." This is an informal monthly meeting of about 10 employees with a top executive from your company. The purpose: to help the employees learn about the organization's most recent financial performance, such as the latest quarterly results. Encourage participants to ask questions about operations and bottom-line concerns. Invite a mix of participants that includes a few managers along with lower-level workers from other departments. This way, these sessions can also serve as a way for employees in different areas and at different levels to mingle.

to teach them how their jobs help the company make money. And 77% of the managers in the same survey agreed.

In the 1990s, the notion of "open-book management" caught fire as a motivational tool. By educating employees to understand your budget and income statements, you can show them the link between their jobs and how the organization delivers products and services that customers value. That can in turn provide the information needed to help employees feel motivated to work smarter and rededicate themselves to operating productively.

While open-book management throughout the company is probably beyond your purview, you can use this method to

Open-book management Educating your employees in the bottom-line operations of your organization by opening the books or teaching them how to read the financial information that your senior executives track. The goal is to help employees learn what they do costs the company and how their work helps the company earn its revenue.

some degree with the group you manage. To do this, begin by identifying a key number that you and your bosses use to measure your unit's performance. In insurance, loss ratios reveal to what extent the business is profitable. Airlines look at load factor (number of seats filled). Banks, mortgage servicing firms, and credit card issuers track delinquencies or default rates. As a new manager, you should find out what figures matter most to higher-ups and make it your business to follow these numbers with keen interest.

The next step is not only to tell employees what numbers you're watching, but also to explain the cash-flow process, the difference between revenue and profit, and how to read an income statement and balance sheet. (If you're not already familiar with these concepts, spend a few hours with your boss to learn what you need to know.)

Finally, establish a clear "line of sight" for employees to connect their jobs to bottom-line benchmarks for the group and the company. A clerk who delivers files may soon appreciate the importance of speed in filling requests; the sooner he can get the file and bring it to a colleague, the faster that colleague can make a decision and respond to a customer. This in turn will increase the customer retention rate, thus saving money because the company doesn't need to attract as many new customers.

Motivating the "Unmotivatable"

You've tried everything. Now you're ready to give up.

Some employees just don't seem to respond to anything. You can compliment them profusely, give them a generous raise, promote them, or simply leave them alone to do their work. Whatever strategy you try to plug into their motivation, you get the same result: a drone who treads water and gives a 70% or 80% effort—enough to meet all job requirements but not nearly sufficient if you want to manage a winning team of exceptional, high-producing superstars.

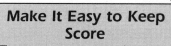

Make It Easy to Keep Score

To motivate your employees to monitor bottom-line numbers, create an easy-to-read scorecard so that everyone can see how they're contributing to a quantifiable organizational goal. Examples include a weekly e-mail update on administrative expenses, profits per employee, or sales growth. By releasing new numbers on an ongoing basis, you can rivet the team's attention on how they can make a difference in the company's performance.

You may be tempted to shrug and say, "I can't figure out what to do with this person, so I'll focus on others." But before you conclude there's nothing else you can do, reconsider the steps you've taken so far. Chances are, whether you were aware of it or not, you've tried to make this person feel motivated by relying on the three P's: pay, praise, and promises (of advancement, more money, more responsibility, etc.). That's not going to work for the toughest 5% of your employees who just won't respond to the same carrots that so often appeal to most others. You need to dig deeper with them.

> ### ⚠ CAUTION! ⚠
> ### Watch Your Mouth
> When you have trouble connecting with an employee, don't publicize it. Rookie managers may vent their frustration by telling coworkers, "I just can't crack that nut" or "I've tried everything, and I guess he's just burned out." When you volunteer such opinions and talk behind the employee's back, you risk alienating him or her further.

To solve the puzzle of helping apathetic employees regain their motivation, resort to more creative measures. Promising advancement won't work, because they've probably topped out and they know it. Promising money won't work, because they've probably pushed their salary grade to its limit and even if they have the skills or credentials to move up, the attitude or desire is not there. Promising accomplishment or power won't work, because they no longer care about leaving their mark or exerting their influence.

Work with each apathetic employee individually. Try introducing change into the employee's routine. Have him or her jettison normal duties and devote more time to challenging projects that harness his or her expertise. Explain that he or she has the talent to make a more significant or lasting contribution to the organization. Add that your unit's success depends on that employee's ability to "give 100%."

I met a new manager who energized a 20-year veteran by saying, "You know, I hate waste—any waste. I don't waste money. I leave a clean plate after every meal. I always recycle.

As I see it, you're this gem who's not shining as much anymore. I can't stand to see so much talent go to waste."

The manager worked with the employee to adjust his job so that he could train newcomers and serve as a kind of in-house consultant. This strategy not only gave the employee a fresh outlook, but it made him dread the idea of squandering his ability and further upsetting his manager.

If the employee once produced better results, appeal to his or her pride. Don't dwell on past glories, but show how much better the present and future can turn out. Like a psychic looking into a crystal ball, describe in exciting detail how the employee's actions today can lead to undeniably huge rewards in the future.

A Picture Is Worth 1,000 Words

Mindy wanted to help Steve feel motivated to regain his momentum as a top salesperson after a prolonged slump. Steve didn't respond to anything: incentive trips, bonuses, the corner office. When Mindy met with him to review yet another dismal month's production, she brought along some old photos of Steve winning company-wide awards at an annual banquet, including the president shaking his hand and a beaming Steve waving from the stage to hundreds of his wildly applauding coworkers. Mindy didn't say much; she just let Steve gaze at the photos. The memories they evoked made Steve reassess his current malaise and rededicate himself to bouncing back.

Manager's Checklist for Chapter 6

❑ Never ask an employee to do something that you wouldn't do yourself.

❑ Use empathy to uncover your employees' hot buttons. Ask lots of questions and dig for clues for what makes them tick.

❑ Help employees feel motivated by measuring performance and praising those who exceed objectives.

❑ Give employees responsibility and listen to their ideas, which encourages them to treat their jobs more seriously.

❏ Teach your team to link their jobs to the bottom line. Apply "open-book management" techniques so that they can examine the same numbers as you and your bosses do.

❏ Connect with the "unmotivatables" by assigning them special projects and allowing them to teach and train others in their area of expertise.

Dishing Out Criticism

I t's your first few weeks as manager and you're already confronting people problems. You've inherited an employee who
seems predisposed to crack nasty jokes at meetings instead of
communicating in a civil tone. Another staffer refuses to turn in
complete, well-researched reports, preferring to give you a sloppy memo riddled with inaccuracies. Finally, a loudmouth mail-
room clerk stomps around all day radiating such anger that
you're concerned a fight will break out.

All these employees need constructive criticism from you.
Yes, *criticism*. If that word sounds harsh, it doesn't have to be. A
big part of your new job as manager is to let your workers know
what they're doing wrong and how they can improve. The negative rap on criticism has less to do with what you say than the
attitude you say it with. If employees come to know that the
criticism you offer is to help them improve, not make yourself
look good at their expense, then they're more likely to listen
and make the changes you suggest.

Let's clear up something right from the start. You want to be
liked by your employees. You've always dreaded supervisors
who judged you relentlessly and who found fault with your
every move. You vowed that when *you* became a manager you

would be different: no incessant criticism, to avoid hurting your employees.

Nice idea. In fact it's a good idea. But the hard truth is you'll often have to criticize your staff. Keeping quiet and hoping problems go away on their own rarely works. In fact, by refusing to tell people what they're doing wrong, you perpetuate a destructive status quo: employees continue to falter and the price of their poor performance or behavior inevitably soars.

You may fear that criticism will unleash negative or self-defeating feelings among subordinates and that their morale will plummet. That will happen only if you criticize thoughtlessly. You will learn in this chapter that if you express yourself clearly and diplomatically, you need not leave lasting scars. Instead, you can build a relationship based on the understanding that what you're doing is helping your employees learn to improve. You're not there to be a roadblock, but a facilitator whose job it is to make sure things go right and don't go wrong.

At the other extreme, you may fear for your own hide if you dare criticize a strong-willed, sharp-tongued veteran. Some new managers tell me they are intimidated by their most vocal, opinionated, and charismatic employees. It's that much harder to give corrective feedback to someone who seems impervious to management.

As you read the techniques that follow, remember that your employees expect to get feedback from you. They know they're not perfect and they know that as their manager it's your job to point out ways for them to do better. As much as you may not like to criticize, realize that

> **Should I Keep Quiet?**
>
> Smart Managing When you're weighing whether to criticize an employee, follow this procedure. Imagine it's six months later and you haven't said a word. What's the worst that can happen? If an individual's bad habits or unacceptable attitude can wreak havoc on your unit, then you may conclude it's smarter to act now than to keep quiet. But if taking the long view helps you realize the issue is relatively minor and may take care of itself, then perhaps you can let yourself off the hook and not criticize.

it's a skill, like negotiating or public speaking. The more times you do it (when it's necessary), the easier it becomes.

Focus on Performance, Not Personality

This chapter opened with examples of three employees who cry out for criticism. It would be easy to say to them, "Your tasteless jokes aren't appropriate" or "Your memos are too sloppy" or "You look so angry today." Easy, but wrong.

The right way to criticize is to focus on observable actions, not attitudes. Instead of saying, "Your tasteless jokes aren't appropriate," say, "When Eleanor suggested a new formula for computing these accounts, your response about her 'dumb math' was inappropriate." And rather than say, "You look so angry today," ask, "Why did you snarl and speak so loudly to that temp?"

By limiting your criticism to what you can see with your own eyes, you refrain from judgments that can trigger the defensive reflex (see Chapter 4). Most people will instinctively defend themselves if you attack their personality or deliver unfair or inflated criticism that moves beyond what's measurable or observable.

Consider the last time you criticized an employee. One measure of your success is whether you were interrupted. If your staffer seemed to listen and let you finish, then that's a small victory. At least you didn't trigger a defensive reaction in the other person the moment you started to talk. But if the person cut you off and started defending, denying, or otherwise punching holes in your comments, you may want to rethink your choice of

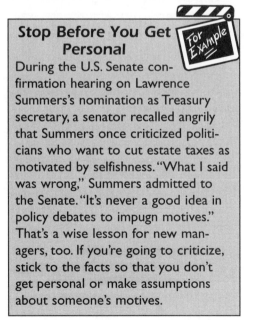

Stop Before You Get Personal

During the U.S. Senate confirmation hearing on Lawrence Summers's nomination as Treasury secretary, a senator recalled angrily that Summers once criticized politicians who want to cut estate taxes as motivated by selfishness. "What I said was wrong," Summers admitted to the Senate. "It's never a good idea in policy debates to impugn motives." That's a wise lesson for new managers, too. If you're going to criticize, stick to the facts so that you don't get personal or make assumptions about someone's motives.

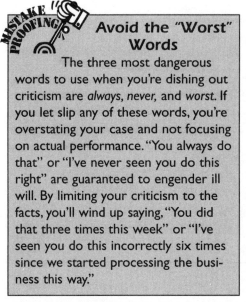

Avoid the "Worst" Words

The three most dangerous words to use when you're dishing out criticism are *always, never,* and *worst.* If you let slip any of these words, you're overstating your case and not focusing on actual performance. "You always do that" or "I've never seen you do this right" are guaranteed to engender ill will. By limiting your criticism to the facts, you'll wind up saying, "You did that three times this week" or "I've seen you do this incorrectly six times since we started processing the business this way."

words, your tone, and/or your approach.

Another example of poor wording is to follow the word "you" with a negative. For instance, saying, "You didn't do that the way I asked" or "You won't listen to reason" will inflame tensions and leave employees feeling shaken and resentful. New managers who are not accustomed to criticizing subordinates often wind up sounding accusatory when they're trying to assert their authority.

A sure way to talk your way into trouble is to make sweeping generalizations or value judgments when you criticize. One reason to describe actions and performance rather than intangibles such as attitude and personality traits is that you'll steer clear of the gross exaggerations and often irrelevant and even dangerous judgmental comments.

You'll know you're on shaky ground if you overuse the words *is* and *are* when referring to the employee (as in "Gene, you are wrong").

In mathematics, *is* means *equals* (e.g., two plus two is four). That's why it pays to avoid *is* and *are* when you criticize; otherwise you wind up equating the person with an undesirable characteristic. And that's a sure sign you're discussing personality or resorting to generalizations rather than dealing with concrete performance issues.

Descriptions Versus Inferences

With all these warnings about words to avoid when you're criticizing employees, you may figure it's almost impossible to say anything safe that will sound supportive and nonthreatening. Actually, it's easy to level with someone in a fair, unbiased tone: just say what you see.

When you describe what you can see, your eyes become cameras. You're taking visual snapshots of your employees' actions. Your words help paint an image that's crisp, clear, and true, free from ambiguities, interpretations, or exaggerations. Better yet, you ensure that your criticism flows from solid empirical evidence rather than vague or biased accusations.

You may be thinking, "Of course I describe behavior when I criticize. There's no other way to do it." But the problem is that managers may confuse *descriptions* with *inferences*. Words such as *careless, temperamental, lazy, self-righteous, arrogant,* and *sloppy* do not reveal anything about an individual's actions, only what can be inferred from a few incidents. Managers who lack precise communication skills may rely on judgment-laden words when they criticize and fail to substantiate their concerns.

> **Inference** Conclusion derived from events, behaviors, or actions. Inferences allow you to jump from one statement that may be true to another that you consider true, but careful listeners may reject your reasoning.

Let's take three examples. If you witnessed an employee get into three arguments today, that's observable behavior that you may want to criticize. But if you say, "You're belligerent today," that's an inference that will probably lead to yet another argument! (The employee may simply have been passionately supporting the com-

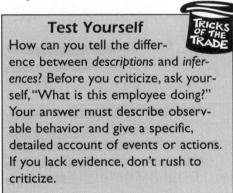

> **Test Yourself**
>
> How can you tell the difference between *descriptions* and *inferences*? Before you criticize, ask yourself, "What is this employee doing?" Your answer must describe observable behavior and give a specific, detailed account of events or actions. If you lack evidence, don't rush to criticize.

pany's objectives.) Similarly, if you say, "I've seen you walk down the hall with your head down, refuse to say hello to anyone, and repeatedly give only the barest one-word answers to customers' questions," that's better than saying, "You seem down, and your moodiness concerns me." And if you notice an employee returning from a two-hour lunch break, you may think of that person as "irresponsible" or "slacking off." However, your criticism should deal only with that observable action, and not go beyond or beneath that action to generalize or draw inferences. By describing only what you see, you can avoid making inferences that could prove wrong. If you approach the employee and say, "You left for lunch two hours ago, right?" you may learn that he was delayed by a serious accident.

> **⚠ CAUTION!**
> ### Descriptions Can Still Sting
> Descriptions are clear, but not necessarily more pleasant than inferences. Even if you say what you see, your employees might guess at what inferences you might be drawing and feel angry or threatened. Nevertheless, it's safer and smarter to refrain from judgments and simply report what actions you observed. You can always simply remind the employee, "I'm concerned about this behavior. Let's focus on that. My goal is for us to work together so you do your job well and I do mine."

Descriptions and inferences can work together when you want to give feedback. If you're still getting to know your employees, don't assume they can figure out what conclusion you're drawing when you merely say what you see. You may want to lead with a description and then follow up with an inference.

Let's say you tell one of your clerks, "Earlier today you took work from Ron's desk and started processing it when you finished going through your work." That statement alone doesn't mean much. Your employee will wonder, "Am I being criticized? Is the boss upset with me? What's going on?" You need to draw an inference to drill home your point.

"That's the kind of initiative I like to see!" assumes a positive motivation and labels this behavior as desirable.

"It's not right for you to snoop around someone else's desk and take things without their permission, even if your intentions are good" indicates that you're not pleased, although you avoid any negative inferences and even allow for good intentions.

Express Criticism as a Question

To make your criticism more palatable to employees, you may want to present it as a question and let them discover for themselves what's wrong. This tactic works especially well with high-ego performers who automatically resist any input they perceive as negative.

When John Calley ran Warner Bros. movie studio in the late 1970s, he had to tell writer/director Irwin Allen that his latest script, "The Walter Syndrome," was terrible. But Calley knew Allen would not accept criticism. So when Allen said, "Take your best shot," Calley didn't go for the bait. Instead, he said, "Irwin, I wouldn't presume to talk story with you, because of who you are—because you are Irwin Allen. I am just not that brazen."

"I understand," Allen replied.

Calley said that instead he would like to ask one question.

"I can't say I'm not intrigued," Allen said. "What is the question?"

"My question is this. Would Cecil B. De Mille have made 'The Walter Syndrome'?"

At that moment, Allen dropped the script into the trash and declared it "a closed issue."

Calley's ability to ask a penetrating question saved him from having to criticize Allen's work. It helped Allen realize that his script wasn't worthy of one of the greatest movie makers of the century—without Calley having to utter even one critical comment.

You can borrow Calley's shrewd technique when you're managing your staff, although in most cases you'll need to offer at least some description before you ask your question. Strive to couple a succinct descriptive comment with a fair, unbiased question. The question should present the employee with a

Criticize Without Criticism

When Mark's employee failed to meet a key deadline, Mark was tempted to say, "I never missed a deadline when I had your job. Now that I'm a manager, I'm not going to tolerate it when my staff can't deliver on time!" But Mark thought better of that aggressive approach. Instead, he used a one-two punch of a description followed by a question. "Last Friday, we agreed you would complete this task by today at 9:00 a.m. It's now noon. Can we talk about what to do when it becomes apparent you can't meet deadlines we set together?" This opens the door to better communication, and the employee may give the manager information he or she can use to get rid of obstacles that prevent Mark (and perhaps other employees) from meeting a deadline.

chance to evaluate his or her action.

As a new manager, you may want to use role reversal as a way to avoid direct criticism of your employees. Here's how:

1. Schedule a private meeting in your office with your employee.
2. When the employee arrives, invite him or her to sit in your chair while you sit in the visitor's chair.
3. From your visitor's seat, ask, "What would you say if you were in my shoes and I had to criticize you for what happened?"
4. Stay silent. Let the employee respond. Some subordinates will prove so rough in their self-criticism that you need not add a word.

A manager at a nonprofit agency successfully used this strategy when her aide, Gary, consistently arrived at work late and didn't respond to repeated requests to show up on time. She had Gary sit in her chair and asked him, "You know how much I need you here at 8:30 every morning. I've tried everything, but in the last week you haven't made it in on time once. What would you say if you were me?"

Gary tried to stall, hoping his boss would continue. She did not. So he started talking, firing off excuse after excuse. Finally, he started to feel embarrassed by his behavior. So he disciplined himself by saying, "I see there's no good excuse for such a lousy track record of coming in late. If I don't make it in on time at least 90% of the time over the next six months, this should affect my performance review and possibly jeopardize the promotion I'm shooting for."

Gary's hard-nosed response impressed his boss. By having him assess his own actions, she made him aware that they were unacceptable without lashing out at him. Sometimes you'll find that employees are harder on themselves than you would be. In that case, you can lighten what they suggest as an enforcement mechanism, and you both feel better about things.

Aside from reducing the amount of stinging criticism you must level at employees, questions also save you from babbling. Many new managers tend to express criticism by talking so much that they leave their employee feeling like a scolded preschooler. Strive to establish a speak-listen rhythm in this kind of conversation so that you don't wind up repeating yourself and using language that's unduly harsh.

Questions also help you avoid lapsing into a lecturing mode. The more you discuss how "unhappy" you are or how vital it is that "screw-ups not occur on my watch," the more you'll shake your employee's confidence and willingness to improve. You may feel you've gotten something off your chest, but the other person will walk away like a wounded animal or simply assume you're an overly critical adversary rather than a decent boss.

What's worse, if you talk too much, you risk coming across like an amateur psychologist. You may start dishing out diagnoses that attempt to explain why an employee isn't performing better, ranging from "a negative, destructive attitude" to "a stubborn insistence to do things your way." That's going beyond description to get into inferences. And the more you talk, the more likely you will say something that will antagonize your staffers and kill any hopes of giving constructive, well-received criticism.

Connect Past to Future

New managers often think criticism consists of explaining something that someone did wrong. That's only partially correct.

In fact, there's another stage to effective criticism: showing
your employee how to improve in the future. You need to mix
your analysis of past actions with a forward-looking prescription
for how the individual can perform better. For instance, telling
your aide that he didn't do a good job setting priorities doesn't
help him organize his time better. You need to suggest steps he
can take from now on to accomplish more pressing tasks in a
systematic way.

Simply instructing your employee to do better won't suffice.
"You've got to shape up!" comes across more as a vague
threat than a rallying cry that will raise the worker's
spirits—and such a rallying cry has little practical
effect: the employee really has no direction on what
behaviors to change or how to change them.
Instead, prod the individual to draft an action plan
that gives a step-by-step process for fixing what's
broken. Have your employee write down possible solution steps and

Smart Managing

You Pick the Solution

Before you criticize someone for poor performance,
identify at least three specific steps
that he or she can take to improve.
These can include finding new ways
to work, modifying existing jobs to
eliminate waste, or committing to
doing the same task in a more com-
prehensive manner. That way, you can
follow up your criticism of past
actions by saying, "Now it's up to you
to learn from this and improve. Here
are some possible ways to do that."

work together to finalize an approach that both of you think will
lead to the necessary improvement.

By directing the employee to think in terms of positive
change, you make your criticism constructive. Labeling someone's work as "bad" or "leaves a lot to be desired" is like the
kiss of death. But if you say, "That work didn't add much value
for our team. In the future, develop your ideas more fully with
examples, projections, and at least some consideration of the

down side," you provide guidance to help the employee improve.

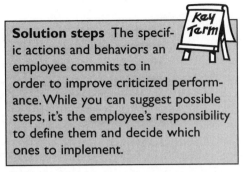

Solution steps The specific actions and behaviors an employee commits to in order to improve criticized performance. While you can suggest possible steps, it's the employee's responsibility to define them and decide which ones to implement.

The danger of dwelling on past failings without tying them to future improvements is that you can leave your employees feeling angry and unsure of their ability. They may start avoiding you, figuring that keeping a low profile will lower the odds that you'll criticize them. And they may try to avoid resuming the work that you criticized, fearing that they just can't "get it right." When you criticize an employee, you need to leave him or her feeling a sense of hope that the next time will be better and that the two of you have agreed on solution steps that make sense. You don't want your criticism to kill the employee's desire to do it again, but better.

Avoid Criticism That Bites Back

We've already warned you that it's dangerous to attack someone's personality when you criticize. Just stick to specific behavior and you improve your chances of having a positive impact.

But that's not the only pitfall of dishing out criticism. New managers face many other dangers when they decide to make an employee aware that there's a performance-related problem he or she needs to improve. Here are five examples of mistakes to avoid:

1. Applying the "sandwich" technique. Some school teachers are taught to give children criticism by mixing good comments with bad ones. Youngsters are more open to negative feedback if it's blended with compliments, according to conventional wisdom. While that may prove true for 7-year-olds, it's not necessarily a smart way to handle your employees. If you sandwich something bad between two slices of praise, most workers will see through your ploy and dwell solely on the criticism. Your positive remarks will sound forced, like you're applying a technique. Example: "You're very bright, Alex, but you're too arrogant. You rub people the wrong way, and you tend to alienate your teammates. I know you're conscientious, and that's something I admire about you." It's a safe bet that Alex will walk away thinking "I'm arrogant?" "I rub people the wrong way?" "I alienate my teammates?" rather than "It's nice to know my boss thinks I'm bright and conscientious." Always look for opportunities to praise, but make it genuine. When you praise, don't detract from it by tossing in some criticism that drowns it out. And remember, generalizations in compliments as well as criticisms are less helpful than focusing on specifics.

2. Letting the blind lead the blind. Never criticize what you don't understand. New managers may assume it's their job to point out employees' flaws and correct them, even if they don't really know what they're talking about. This often happens when a technician gets promoted into a position of people management. The newly installed manager notices an employee who's struggling with a new software program, so he criticizes the worker for "doing it wrong" and then says, "Here, let me show you how to do it right." After a few minutes of fruitless experimentation, the manager realizes he has no idea what he's doing. He's winging it. Had the manager refrained from criticizing and instead tried to fiddle with the program alongside the employee so that they could learn together, they could have bonded a bit without undermining the subordinate's confidence.

3. Hogging the spotlight. If you get nervous when you're about to criticize someone, you may tend to alleviate your jitters by talking about a subject you're much more comfortable with: you. Rather than describe your concern clearly and propose a solution that helps your employee perform better, you may lapse into a monologue in which you discuss your own upset feelings, worries, or experiences that may or may not relate to the issue at hand. Don't focus on yourself; stick to your agenda.

In a role-play during one of my management training seminars, I asked a new manager to practice criticizing an employee. But he didn't talk about the other person's work product; instead, he spent five minutes repeating how "let down" and "dismayed" he felt in dealing with his employee. Finally, I said, "You've made it clear how *you* feel. Now give your employee some helpful criticism, or you'll risk dominating the conversation."

4. Making a spectacle. Never criticize an employee in front of others. Remember that you want to leave the individual feeling confident and motivated to improve. If you express your concerns in public, you can embarrass and even humiliate the person you're trying to help. Some managers mistakenly think it's fine to criticize someone with others watching—that teaching a lesson in front of onlookers increases the odds it will sink in. That's playing with fire. Criticism is hard enough for most people to take in private when communicated in a supportive manner. But if you deliver it in a crowded staff meeting, you're almost guaranteed to create tension. Even seemingly harmless comments such as "That's not how we do things around here" or "You're not trying very hard, are you?" can hurt and send a message that you're more of a harsh judge than a judicious manager.

5. Rushing to advise. There's a subtle difference between making a suggestion and giving advice. Suggestions offer hints, insights, or observations that the listener can choose to embrace or reject. Advice involves telling someone how to solve a problem. It can include specific steps, actions, and instructions. When you're criticizing employees, don't hop right into giving advice. First, pinpoint the action that you observed and describe it fully and accurately. Then show your interest in the worker's point of view, asking questions and maintaining a balanced speak-listen ratio so that you're both contributing to the conversation. Ideally, you want your employee to ask, "Say, do you have any ideas on how I can improve?" That gives you an opening to advise. But in most cases, it won't prove so easy to bark out do-this, do-that commands. That's why you should lay off the advice and stick to safe suggestions that enable employees to think for themselves and draw their own conclusions.

Even if you steer clear of the five problem areas outlined above, you still need to pay attention to your tone and body language. Don't raise your voice or sound upset when you criticize. Speak in your normal, conversational style. In fact, it's fine to radiate a dose of enthusiasm when you criticize. That's right—you don't need to dread what you say and wear your "this is dead serious" face. As long as your comments are sincere and do not blame, there's no reason to sound hesitant, stern, or downbeat.

Don't frown, grimace, or otherwise appear gloomy or annoyed. If you're nervous, you may unleash your anxiety by speaking in a more tense or agitated manner. Control your fear so that your nervousness does not envelop the room.

The safest and smartest criticism comes across as a gentle form of supportive, well-intentioned awareness-raising, not as a red flag frantically waving in front of an employee's panicked and bewildered face. You want to share observations and seek information to help your employee succeed, not assert your superiority by proclaiming, "I told you that wouldn't work" or "You're just too impatient and aggressive." Like a friendly but curious detective, you want to investigate behavior rather than take positions and assign right-wrong labels prematurely.

TRICKS OF THE TRADE

Use "ICE" When You Criticize

Here's an easy three-step process to help you criticize better. First, greet your employee and make an "I" statement, such as "I have a problem" or "I'm concerned about something, and it involves your performance." Second, contrast the type of action you need with what the employee's doing. Example: "I need to know the numbers on the weekly activity report are completely accurate, but for the past month I've found several errors." Third, ask for an explanation in a nonthreatening tone, such as "Could you help me understand what's going on?" or "Explain to me what's happening." Through the ICE approach (*I* statements-Contrast behavior-Explain), you can work with the employee to hash out solution steps.

Manager's Checklist for Chapter 7

❏ Focus your criticism on an employee's specific behavior or actions, not on personality.

❏ Report "just the facts" by saying what you see. Don't assign blame or label the behavior.

❏ Avoid using the words *always, never,* and *worst.* And don't follow "you" with a negative such as "You didn't ..." or "You won't ...."

❏ Ask questions when you criticize, to encourage your employees to do your work for you. Prod them to evaluate their performance honestly in a nonthreatening atmosphere.

❏ Provide forward-looking criticism that ties past actions to future improvements.

❏ Never criticize what you do not understand.

❏ Speak in a supportive, conversational tone when you criticize. Don't raise your voice or sound upset.

Discipline That Pays Off

When Dave learned that one of his employees had lied about some lost invoices, he knew he had to figure out a fair but tough way to punish such misbehavior. But he had no idea what to do.

Should he berate the individual and demand an apology? Or should he go a step further and write up the incident to add to the personnel file? Then there was the harsh step of employment probation—a more formal and high-stakes way of sending a message that Dave would not tolerate lying.

Most new managers have no blueprint to follow for disciplining employees. It's almost always a judgment call, and that makes it a hornet's nest in more ways than one. If you're too soft, you risk inviting more of the same kind of unacceptable actions. If you're too hard-nosed, you can gain a reputation as an inflexible tyrant who goes overboard and has no sense of perspective. And if you ignore it entirely or delay deciding how to respond, you undermine the whole process by waiting too long.

What's at Stake?

The biggest mistake rookie managers make when having to discipline their staff is they react impulsively. Rather than planning what they want to say and do based on an objective analysis of the facts, they lash out and let their emotions interfere. Instead of isolating the specific wrongdoing and determining why it matters, they rush to put their foot down because they feel an employee has betrayed their trust, a costly miscue will slow the unit's progress, or they're simply fed up and need to unleash their frustration.

To avoid reacting emotionally, make sure you know what's at stake before you exert discipline. Ask yourself three sets of questions:

1. **Repercussions.** What short- and long-term harm can this behavior cause? Could the employee have foreseen such harm?

2. **Rationale.** Are there mitigating factors? For example, did the individual have at least some positive reasons or valid motives for the behavior? Was the employee under the impression there was a greater good to be gained that justified the wrongdoing?

3. **Lessons.** What messages do you want to send through your choice of discipline? Do other employees and/or bosses care about this situation? Do they clearly know to what extent and why the employee's actions were wrong? Or do you need to explain?

Many new managers lack an institutional history. They don't realize that other managers before them have probably dealt with the same or similar disciplinary challenges and that the *precedent chain* can provide helpful clues on how to respond. By investigating how such problems have been handled before, you can apply consistent punishment that fits with your organizational culture.

Never view a single incident in isolation,

> **Precedent chain** A sequence of disciplinary measures that you and/or your predecessors have taken for the same type of offense. By linking the chain of events that have come before, you can use precedent to guide your decision on applying the appropriate level of discipline.

detached from other types of problems. You can discipline an employee for hundreds of reasons, but they're almost all related in some way to what's come before. If possible, contact the previous manager to discuss how such matters were handled. Also check with a representative from human resources and—for serious incidents—an employment lawyer. Dig to determine how the past should influence your present course of action.

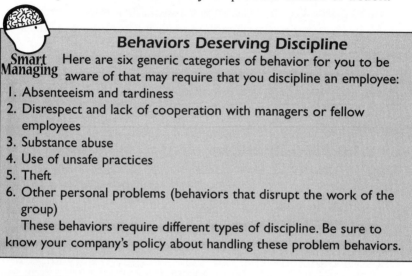

Behaviors Deserving Discipline

Smart Managing   Here are six generic categories of behavior for you to be aware of that may require that you discipline an employee:

1. Absenteeism and tardiness
2. Disrespect and lack of cooperation with managers or fellow employees
3. Substance abuse
4. Use of unsafe practices
5. Theft
6. Other personal problems (behaviors that disrupt the work of the group)

These behaviors require different types of discipline. Be sure to know your company's policy about handling these problem behaviors.

Disciplining the Uncooperative Pest

Lucky Stan. During his first month as a new supervisor, he didn't have to discipline any of his employees.

Yet one customer-service rep soon became increasingly surly and unresponsive. Eventually, he refused to follow orders. But rather than say "No," he simply laughed at Stan's requests and said, "Yeah, you better get out your whip and use that wet noodle to get me into shape."

Stan tried to reason with this person to no avail. Then he issued a few verbal warnings that bordered on threats (e.g., "If you don't shape up, I'm going to ..."), but his words seemed to fall on deaf ears. He began to feel as if his authority was on the line. That's when I was brought in to advise him.

Stan's first priority, I told him, was to avoid threats he didn't

intend to back up and instead communicate with steely determination and undeniable firmness. I advised him to speak in a
concise, confident, and direct tone. That meant choosing his
words more carefully and saying less but making it count more.

The best disciplinarians don't babble or repeat themselves in
desperation; instead, they muzzle a malcontent with a stern look
and a succinct warning that they utter slowly, such as "Stop
right there" or "Hold on now." They emphasize each word so
that the message sinks in.

In Stan's case, the next time his employee attempted to
reject or laugh off an instruction, he needed to put an end to
such behavior. While listening often makes sense, a manager
cannot remain passive when a subordinate continues to make
inflammatory or insulting remarks.

"Make it clear you're serious," I told Stan, "and that you
won't tolerate any more of this by explaining what needs to happen, and what the consequences will be if it doesn't happen."

We practiced nonverbal cues that would help shut down inappropriate behavior, such as putting a hand up with his palm facing the employee as a signal to stop talking. We also examined
the precedent chain at his company to decide what punishments
would unfold if the behavior didn't improve, ranging from written
warnings to probation to possible termination. Finally, we alerted
Stan's boss of the situation so that everyone agreed on the best
way to proceed. (New
managers shouldn't hesitate
to inform their boss of a
disciplinary problem to
enlist the necessary sup-
port to clamp down on the
undesirable behavior.)

How to Play Referee

If you supervise just one
individual, then you only
have to worry about

**Don't Take
the Bait**

Don't let your dislike of
certain employees interfere with the
way you discipline them. New managers can let difficult employees pull
their strings and goad them into
exploding or otherwise saying things
they regret later. If you're angry or
extremely irritable, detach yourself
and regain your composure before
you discuss disciplinary steps.

disciplining that person. But if you manage more than one employee, you may face off against two troublemakers who both get into a mess. In those situations, you become a mediator as well as a manager. You must play the role of the unbiased, dispassionate referee.

Before you can mete out punishment, you need to investigate what happened and help bickering workers understand each other's position. That's a tall order, especially when tensions run high and rivals vie for your support. In these situations, discipline goes hand in hand with addressing misunderstandings and improving trust among your team.

Following a fair, systematic approach can ensure that you do not talk yourself into trouble and overstep your bounds. Here's a six-step process to help you discipline warring employees without having to bark orders like a tyrant.

> **Smart Managing**
>
> ## One at a Time
>
> When you need to discipline more than one employee, it's usually best to do so in private. Hold one-on-one discussions with each wrongdoer and emphasize how his or her performance must improve. Keep each conversation confidential. Disciplining employees should rarely be a public affair, because you want each individual to feel the full force of your actions—not bond with other employees who are in the same boat. And you never want to humiliate someone in front of coworkers.

1. Get "I" statements. Gather both employees in a room and ask each of them to state the problem. Have them start with "I" statements, such as "I did ..." or "As I see it ..."—e.g., "I did everything I could to warn Wally about this, but he didn't listen to me" or "I felt I had no choice but to cut corners because Gene was making us fall behind schedule." "You" statements blaming the other person bring out defense mechanisms that do not help solve the problem.

2. Trade sides. Now ask each employee to state the problem *from the other's point of view*. They should start by saying, "The way [coworker] sees it ... " It may take a few tries before each person can step into the other person's shoes and explain the situation in a satisfactory manner. Have each participant confirm the accuracy of the other's restatement before you move to the next stage.

3. Reinforce mutual needs. Get both employees to nod and think, "Yes, that's important." Establish a base of agreement, a bedrock of understanding that both parties cannot help but acknowledge. "You both need to find a way to work together" or "All our jobs are at risk in this merger" can unify adversaries and refocus everyone's attention on mutual goals.

4. Collaborate on a solution. Ask each worker to propose positive, productive steps to help everyone attain the mutual goals you've identified. If they're hesitant or simply don't have any sensible ideas, give them a day or two to ponder the problem and reconvene. Make it clear you expect both employees to issue specific recommendations, and that they will need to work together to implement a solution that all of you help create.

5. Discipline. Now's the time to penalize the employees or at least lay out the consequences of their actions. First, arrange to see each employee privately. You might want to break for lunch and then allot 10 minutes for a closed-door meeting with each participant. Use phrases such as "In view of your efforts today to work together, I'm going to be lenient" or "Normally, I'd dock your pay but given your fine input and your willingness to learn from this, I'll go easy on you." (Make sure that the harsher discipline is a possibility in terms of company policy and the law. Otherwise, employees may call your bluff—or at least lose some respect for you.) This way, you still exert discipline—but it comes across as a somewhat gentle, positive outgrowth of your employees' collaboration rather than as a stinging rebuke that breeds resentment.

6. Set a timetable. Conclude by mapping out the implementation of your employees' problem-solving scheme. Set preliminary and final deadlines to produce results. If you're punishing them, apply a time frame to this as well so that they'll know when they've finishing paying for their misbehavior.

When you're disciplining an employee, keep the focus on that individual's performance. Don't let the worker shift the discussion to another person or try to pin blame on someone else. If you've already gathered the facts and confirmed them with all the par-

Put It in Writing

For the first step of asking employees to give "I" statements, you may want to have them write down their remarks. Many workers will describe their behavior more accurately on paper than if they just talk about it. That's because they can inject ambiguities into their speech that they would be more reluctant to express in print. Plus, if a conflict arises about the facts, at least you'll have written summaries to compare each individual's version of events. Be sure to ask for the assumptions each employee made that caused them to behave as they did. It's often the case that conflicts are the result of people working from conflicting assumptions.

ties, then there's no reason to rehash these issues. Tell the employee, "We're not here to talk about others. We're here to discuss *your* role and agree on the consequences of *your* actions."

Finally, don't expect everyone to accept your punishment with grace and good cheer. Discipline is an art, not a science. There's no single right answer in deciding how to respond to misbehavior. Sometimes you'll wind up being too soft; in other instances, you'll overreact and kick yourself later for blowing a relatively minor error out of proportion. And even if you're scrupulously fair in choosing how to discipline, your employees may not see it that way.

Don't fret if you feel like you've misfired in weighing how hard to put your foot down. Just try to evaluate to what extent your disciplinary actions produce the desired long-term effect in your employees. It's a sad but true fact of management that you'll have plenty of other chances to practice how you exert discipline. On the other hand, you do not want to be perceived as unjust or out to get employees. Your job is to create a work environment that encourages a disciplined and productive work force in the best sense of those terms. If you make a mistake in dealing with an employee, it's OK to admit it, explain your reasoning, and use that as a lesson for knowing how to deal with similar situations in the future.

When to Write Up an Employee

Ruth learned that one of her employees said to a coworker, "That Ruth is really screwing us. She's a liar. Let's teach her a lesson and go over her head."

Like most bosses, you would probably be hurt and angry if you heard about such a vicious comment. But Ruth didn't sit and stew. Instead, she wrote up her employee for insubordination.

"The formality of putting a memo in this employee's personnel file struck me as appropriate under the circumstances," Ruth told me. "I wanted to send a message that you just don't talk that way about your boss and get away with it. I want my people to know if they're going to be nasty and bad-mouth me or any other manager, then their behavior will be officially documented."

Fair enough. But rather than rush to write up an employee, as Ruth did, it's often wise to treat this form of written discipline more carefully. After all, whenever you scold someone in writing, you magnify the incident by memorializing it in that individual's personnel file. It becomes a permanent piece of history, a black mark that will taint the employee's name over the long haul. While it underscores the seriousness of someone's behavior, it comes at a cost. You sow the seeds of mutual distrust and leave a trail of lasting ill will.

Here are three tests to help you weigh whether it's wise to discipline employees in writing:

1. **Did you already hold a face-to-face meeting?** Ruth was so furious that she didn't bother to contact the employee and ask, "Do you have a beef with me?" She assumed that what she had

heard through the grapevine was true and she acted accordingly.

Never discipline others as an emotional reaction to upsetting news. It's a safe bet you'll either overdo it and exaggerate the importance of what happened or lose sight of the work-related issue and take the whole incident personally. New managers are especially susceptible to this dangerous rush to judgment, because they're new to the discipline game.

You must meet with the employee at some point, so you might as well talk it over and hear his or her version of events *before* rather than *after* you put anything in writing. Through a forthright, cool-headed dialogue, you can learn information that will provide a more complete understanding of the employee's motives and intentions. This in turn can help you figure out how to proceed.

2. **Do you know the full story?** Disciplining an employee is hard enough without having to separate fact from fiction. In many disputes, ambiguities make it hard for a manager to assign blame with any accuracy. If everyone agrees on the events in question—and those events clearly violated your company's policies—then you're on safe ground writing a disciplinary memo. And if you have evidence to prove what happened, such as a videotape that shows a theft in progress, then that's even better.

But in many cases, confirming the facts is an exercise in futility. No matter how diligently you try to get to the bottom of

---

⚠ CAUTION!

Discipline Without Risk

Don't make a final decision about writing up an employee until you're absolutely certain about what happened. Your credibility is on the line, so make sure you're right. Cross-check every relevant fact with the parties involved so that you're sure you have correct information. If that's impossible, but you still feel compelled to take some kind of strong-willed action, sit down with the employee suspected of wrongdoing and talk it out. Note whether the employee seems tense or defensive; making someone squirm can prove its own kind of tough discipline. Rather than try to know the unknowable, explain the levels of punishment that *any* worker can expect for certain types of wrongdoing.

a conflict or seek to explain an otherwise competent employee's lapse in judgment, you may never know what really happened or whom to believe.

3. Is the employee a repeat offender? Say you've already tried gentler forms of discipline, such as issuing oral warnings and denying the individual minor privileges. But the employee continues to perform unacceptably and shows no sign of trying to improve. Here's when it's wise to assert your authority.

A bluntly worded memo can drill home your displeasure with an employee's actions. Using phrases such as "this behavior is unacceptable and will not be tolerated in the future" or "this puts you on notice that any further violation of company policy will result in further disciplinary action" can send a chill down an employee's spine.

Once you write such a memo, wait a day before you send it. Reread it to ensure you stick to the core issue and that you clearly explain what the employee did wrong, why it's wrong, and what will happen if such behavior continues.

Delete any inflammatory language or comments that detract from your main message. For example, don't write, "I suspected that you would not heed my last warning" or "Your actions reveal an immaturity that has hurt your reputation in this organization." Such comments threaten to open a Pandora's box that's best left sealed. What's worse, an employee will probably dwell on these sentences and disregard the rest.

Getting Personal

You might as well learn this lesson now rather than later: it's unwise to turn a disciplinary message into a personal attack against the employee. That's one of those basic truths that most managers know, but remarkably few follow.

Rookie managers may think they're just focusing on faulty, substandard performance when they discipline. But then they inject all kinds of inappropriate or overblown remarks that trigger antagonism. This applies to discipline expressed both in print and in person. Here are some examples of how *not* to launch a disciplinary discussion:

- "I'm at my wit's end with you. This just keeps happening, and I'm ready to scream."
- "Your error rate is out of control. You don't seem to be making enough of an effort."
- "I give up trying to figure out your problem. It's beyond me."
- "In all my years of work, I've never faced anyone quite like you."
- "It seems apparent to me you don't treat our performance standards seriously."

Don't laugh. Maybe you wouldn't talk this way, but many otherwise tactful, well-intentioned managers do. Notice that there are a lot of "you" messages in these statements. And though the managers aren't necessarily speaking in an insulting or malicious tone, they may be so nervous or uncomfortable with the prospect of having to discipline someone that they wing it and wind up saying things they regret later.

Aside from the fact that these types of openers instantly turn employees against you, they also signal that you're not in the mood for a fair, balanced dialogue. Instead, they may lead your employee to conclude that you're going to lecture, scold, and pontificate. Such a one-sided conversation is hardly conducive to working together to help a person change his or her behavior in a positive way. And that prospect of hearing their boss rail against them for 10 minutes can prove punishment enough for many employees, especially if they want to give their side of the story.

Don't take pot shots when you discipline. Avoid making innuendoes and trying to analyze *why* an employee has not produced quality work or has not followed the rules. The "why" isn't as important as clearly explaining what the person did and how that action or behavior fell below an acceptable standard.

New managers often wonder how to start a conversation when they must explore the reasons for poor work. The best

Too Much "I"

In her first few months as a manager, Fran could tell Barry's work was slipping. She mentioned casually a few times what she was observing, but now she opted for more formal discussion with Barry. First she rehearsed what she wanted to say: *You're letting me down. I used to work alongside you, so I've seen you at your best. Now whenever I come into your office, you close the window on your computer as if you're hiding something. It's like you'd rather play games than work. What's up?* I warned Fran that this approach wouldn't succeed because it was more about her perception and personal interpretations than the actual areas where Barry failed to meet performance standards. A better approach would be simply to ask Barry what was going on, to get his perspective. Then the two can problem solve to remedy the situation.

strategy is to set a friendly, inquiring tone and establish from the outset that you expect a give-and-take discussion. You might start off with an open-ended question, such as "Ted, you've been here two years now, and I'm curious whether you feel as if you're making progress in your job in finding effective ways to meet our performance standards. How do you think you're doing?"

It's often smart to begin by mentioning how long the individual has been employed at your organization. That instantly provides perspective and shows that you've done some research. It also can put the employee in a reflective or confessional mood. You may hear revealing responses such as a cheerful "Has it been that long!?" or a doleful "Yeah, I have been here a long, long time." Such responses can give a sense of the person's attitude about the job, which can be helpful as you discuss what can be done to turn performance around.

Another benefit of opening the meeting in this manner is that you avoid volunteering your feelings or opinions too soon. You don't want to pounce on the employee from the start by expressing your disappointment or dismay at all that he or she has done wrong. This will inject a needlessly personal, adversarial tone into the discussion.

Beware of getting personal when an employee's attitude rubs you the wrong way. A scowling, sarcastic, or bitter individ-

Doing Your Homework

Before you attempt to discipline someone in person, invest a few minutes to read the employee's personnel file. Prepare some notes that you can refer to during the meeting. They should provide key facts at a glance, such as years/months of employment, past disciplinary problems, past accomplishments, and perhaps a list of previous positions, job titles, and bosses. This fact-finding will boost your confidence and demonstrate that you've taken an interest in the individual—rather than deciding to dish out punishment impulsively.

ual can bring out the worst in you, so it's crucial to stick to the issue at hand and not react negatively to personality traits. Realize that most people don't like to confront their substandard performance; they'd rather pretend as if everything's fine or at least avoid hearing their boss analyze in detail how they're failing. Employees can respond with denial and rebellion—not forthright, chagrined acceptance.

If you try to describe in objective terms how the employee's performance falls below what's acceptable and you're greeted with derision or outright disagreement, then resist the urge to contradict ("No, you're wrong!") or make a personal attack ("Where do you come off saying that to me!?"). Instead, remain dispassionate and say in a nonthreatening tone, "We sure see things differently. Based on my observation and these activity reports, it's clear your performance doesn't meet the standards we've set for the job. Can you figure out why we're apart on this?"

This approach invites a more searching, honest dialogue. Employees will appreciate the chance to state their case, even if you conclude it's built on excuses. By listening patiently, however, you gain credibility and solidify your position as a sensitive, fair-minded boss who doesn't rush to discipline without hearing all sides.

Discipline That Sticks

If you're going to discipline, you might as well make it count. Saying, "I'm unhappy with your work" or "I leave it up to you to

> ### Mild, Medium, and Hot
>
> To avoid making inflammatory remarks that wind up pro-
> voking a personal feud, begin your discussion in a positive
> frame of mind. Banish any thoughts of dread such as "I hate doing this."
> Instead, describe in unambiguous terms what qualifies as satisfactory
> behavior and how the employee's actions have not met this threshold.
> If the employee bristles or fights back, imagine that you can choose
> between a mild, medium, and hot reply. Start with mild. Don't give your-
> self permission to escalate the battle by displaying a medium or hot
> reaction. Think of mild as straightforward and serious communication.
> Medium is stern, and hot is harsh. Medium and hot are likely to pro-
> voke a defensive response—not one that promotes cooperation.

find a way to improve" won't suffice. Such vague comments
rarely lift an individual's performance on their own. You need to
provide more direct, specific guidance.

If you know that a staffer's behavior is unacceptable and
merits punishment of some sort, but you're unsure what's appropriate, then lay out three possible disciplinary steps you can take
and let the employee decide which one applies. For example,
you can say, "Given what you've done, I can either suspend you
for a day, require that you design and lead a training program to
help others not make the same mistake, or simply write you up
and put you on probation. Which one would you choose?"

By allowing the employee to select the specific punishment,
you achieve three goals. First, you increase the odds the individual will rebound from the misbehavior and perform more
effectively in the future. The worker thus becomes a participant
in the disciplinary process, not a spectator awaiting bad news.
Second, you avoid having to decide which course of action to
take. New managers may lack experience with discipline, so by
providing a menu of choices you let yourself off the hook to
some degree. Finally, you can learn more about how an employee thinks by noting which punishment he or she chooses. It's
another way to get to know what makes your staffers tick.

Another approach to put teeth into your discipline is to help
the employee trace a clear deterioration in performance. You

may want to draw a timeline or graph that displays a steady decline in productivity, based on some objective measure such as files processed per day or cases settled per day. Let the facts speak for themselves.

A final word about discipline. Propose a way for the individual to show immediate improvement. Don't just describe what went wrong and why that's unacceptable; insist that you see marked improvement by, say, next Friday—or you will need to take further action. Confirm that the employee understands the gravity of the situation and the need to produce better results or act more professionally *now*—not later. Then when you see improvement, be sure to give the employee some positive feedback. Positive feedback gives employees concrete cues about what you expect from them and encourages them to improve in the direction you're looking for.

Manager's Checklist for Chapter 8

❏ Before you exert discipline, know the repercussions of the misbehavior, the rationale for what happened, and the lessons you want the employee to learn.

❏ Consider precedent when you discipline. Make sure you're being consistent when responding to similar types of wrongdoing.

❏ Discipline in private and focus on the unacceptable actions, performance, or behavior—not personality.

❏ Don't rush to write up an employee. Save this formal option for cases of serious wrongdoing. Then gather facts and listen to all sides before making a judgment.

❏ Always read an employee's personnel file before you discipline.

❏ Give employees a choice of what they think is fair discipline from among three similar types of punishment.

The Organized Manager

Todd's job kept him on the move. As a risk manager for a big corporation, he'd spend most days visiting field offices and inspecting their facilities for safety hazards. He didn't set a specific time for people to expect him at each stop, so he could make his own schedule and show up at branch offices whenever he wanted.

When Todd became a manager, however, he needed to overhaul his whole approach to time management. He had meetings to attend, schedules to stick to and enforce, and activity reports to complete by set deadlines. Suddenly, the clock played a vital role in his daily job. He had to find a way to work more productively and sharpen his organizational skills.

Most new managers experience the same bracing realization. They're usually overwhelmed at first by the amount of work they face, and they wonder how they're supposed to get everything accomplished in an eight- or 10-hour day. Then they gradually find ways to work more efficiently or at least guard their time more carefully to minimize waste.

For many managers, organizing doesn't come naturally. Don't let yourself off the hook that easily. "I'm just not all that efficient" or "Time management isn't my strong suit" are cop-out phrases. You're not born with organizational skills—you develop them. You need to find ways to get more done in less time, and that takes a high degree of awareness.

If you want to hit the ground running as a new manager, take immediate steps to become more organized. The sooner you learn how to increase your productivity, the faster you'll make an impact. Plus, your disciplined time-management skills will set an example for others to follow. You will control the job—not vice versa.

Are You Running on Time?

The first step in sharpening your organizational skills is identifying your work habits. You must become more territorial about how you spend your time, rather than routinely letting events or people take big chunks of your day.

Take the following test to diagnose how well you manage your time and impose order on the chaos of everyday life.

Answer each of the following questions on a 1-to-10 scale, with 1 as "never," 5 as "half the time," and 10 as "always."

Meals. I skip breakfast or lunch because I'm in a rush or too busy to eat. _5_

Deadlines. I miss deadlines or do not complete assignments by the time I promised to. _1_

Down Time. When I've got time to kill, I'll dally and then kick myself later for not using that time more wisely. _1_

Mishaps. When I've lost something like my eyeglasses or my computer crashes, I'll drop everything and focus on the problem—even if it takes an hour or two. _1_

Procrastination. When I dread a task or assignment, I'll repeatedly put it off. _2_

Flexibility. When a sudden crisis needs my attention, I'll shift gears and address it only after I've taken care of other, relatively minor loose ends. _10_

Awareness. I lose track of the time during the work day. _2_

Clutter. I'm unable to work efficiently at my desk because of all the clutter. _1_

Meetings. I spend more time than necessary in meetings. _3_

Scheduling. I overbook myself during the day, which forces me to run late habitually. _1_

Total your score. A result over 60 indicates a serious lack of organization. A score over 80 almost guarantees you won't last long in the management ranks because you're going to operate inefficiently. Most new managers score between 40 and 60, which means they can stand to improve but they're already somewhat organized. If your total falls below 40, then you're off to a great start.

Maximizing Each Hour

If your spouse complains that you're "so protective of your time," that's a red flag in a relationship. It's often better to go with the flow and not worry about zealously guarding every precious moment.

But what works in your personal life may not translate to success in the office. That's because effective managers *must* protect their time. If they don't, they let circumstances control them and then they must struggle to stick to a well-managed plan. Remaining flexible in the face of an emergency is wise, but being too willing to set aside one task for another can leave you not accomplishing anything.

To boost your level of organization, know when you can produce the best results. Most managers can function at their absolute best during a certain hour of the day, whether it's early morning, just before lunch, or the late afternoon when most others have left and there's less noise and distractions. During this "optimal hour," you can concentrate fully, finish what you start, and balance two or three tasks at once.

New managers often assume their optimal hour falls at the end of the day, when their employees have left and they can quietly regroup. But don't confuse your "mop up" time, when you rifle through paperwork, with your peak work period, when you can move beyond your daily chores.

Optimal hour The hour of the work day when you're able to perform most productively, when you're most focused, attentive, and inquisitive. Smart managers reserve this period to tackle their most sensitive, demanding, or dreaded assignments.

To discover your optimal time, take 10 minutes next Sunday night to create a written schedule for the week ahead. Reserve a different one-hour chunk of time for each of the next five days. Example: Monday, 8:00-9:00 a.m.; Tuesday, 10:00-11:00 a.m.; Wednesday, 11:00 a.m.-12:00 p.m.; Thursday, 2:00-3:00 p.m.; Friday, 4:00-5:00 p.m.

Each day, set aside those designated hours for uninterrupted work. Don't take phone calls or see visitors during these times. After you complete each hour, evaluate your productivity. Assign a letter grade (A through F) based on how well you worked, how much you accomplished, and your energy level.

When the week's over, you can tell your optimal hour by analyzing which time received the highest grade. You may want to repeat this process for a second week and experiment with different hours, or try blocking out the same hours again and evaluating whether you gave yourself the same grades for the same times.

> **TRICKS OF THE TRADE**
>
> ### Your Private Time
>
> Once you discover when you can function at your best, don't keep it a secret. Guard this hour religiously. Close your door, post a sign-up sheet to ward off interrupting visitors, and forward your incoming calls. Save your most challenging task for this hour and let everyone know that this time belongs to you.

Invest in the Future

Just as you put aside money in a retirement plan, you should take steps now to become more organized later. Savvy managers lay the groundwork so that when crises inevitably erupt, they're well equipped to stay on track and remain productive. They don't get flustered because they've planned for the unexpected and cut themselves some slack to handle the rush of events.

Here are some strategies to anticipate time wasters and boost your standing as an unflappable, well-organized manager.

Make incremental progress. New managers often schedule their toughest or least liked activities, such as performance reviews or disciplinary meetings, without considering the time they'll need to prepare for such discussions. For example, they may line up a series of appraisals one after another on Monday morning, without factoring in the time they need to review each employee's personnel file and outline what they want to say.

Another mistake is to shrug off upcoming deadlines if there are still at least a few days left. But soon enough, the deadline day arrives and the careless manager must play catch-up at the last minute to get the work done.

A better approach is to organize your time so that you work steadily toward a goal. Commit to making at least some progress early and often, even if you're merely jotting some notes for a meeting that's a week or two away. And if you need to research an issue by talking to colleagues, initiate those calls now. That way, you won't panic if you can't reach them right away or if they're out of the office for a few days.

Make a list for tomorrow, not today. Some managers don't bother to write a daily to-do list, which makes organization almost impossible. Others scribble a few reminders when they arrive in the office every morning, which can induce stress as the phone starts ringing and other fires break out. Within a few minutes of settling down to work, you can be overwhelmed and convinced you'll never find the time to refine your list, much less cross off anything!

The smartest, most efficient managers treat such lists more seriously. They write them the previous night so that they can wake up the next morning knowing what must get done that day. And by composing the list when they're calm and unhurried, they can think more clearly about what must get done and prioritize better.

Prepare to pause. Even the most disciplined managers cannot crank out excellent work for hours on end. Everyone needs a break, or at least a chance to activate different parts of the brain throughout the day. That's why you should allow pockets of down time when planning your day's activities. Budget your time generously so that you're more likely to work ahead of schedule than fall behind.

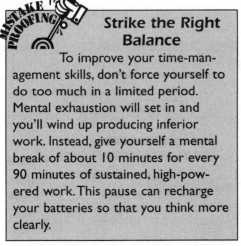

Strike the Right Balance

To improve your time-management skills, don't force yourself to do too much in a limited period. Mental exhaustion will set in and you'll wind up producing inferior work. Instead, give yourself a mental break of about 10 minutes for every 90 minutes of sustained, high-powered work. This pause can recharge your batteries so that you think more clearly.

Pounce on promises. When you tell someone you'll do something, do it now. Don't procrastinate and assume you'll remember it later. New managers often find themselves telling employees, "I don't know, but I'll find out and get back to you." Write down every commitment you make, even if it's as simple as gathering some facts about the company's leave policy or commuting options.

Another benefit of following up on requests is that you avoid making people nag you later. For example, if a colleague proposes a practical pointer on Monday, apply it right away and report back by Friday on what you learned thanks to the suggestion. If you don't initiate this type of progress report, you may be interrupted when the person calls you back to ask if you've acted on the advice yet.

You don't even need to talk to the colleague. To save time, you may want to send an e-mail or leave a message on voice mail during the early morning when you know that person isn't in the office.

Banishing Time Wasters

Organized managers cannot operate on auto-pilot. They must fight off forces that sap their time and energy. If they're too complacent, then they'll wind up reacting to the rush of events rather than imposing some kind of steely discipline on their work day.

The most insidious time wasters are also the hardest to resist. I'll help you overcome three of the toughest threats to maintaining an efficient schedule: engaging in wasteful or annoying conversations, dreading tasks you don't like, and failing to take advantage of pockets of down time.

From "Harmless" Chats to Knock-Down Arguments

Valerie loves to talk. Her employees grumble that she's a compulsive blabbermouth and they try to avoid running into her during the work day. When she corners you, she'll start discussing topics that don't relate to your job—and she'll toss in dozens of long-winded examples or anecdotes on topics far afield from anything you need (or want) to know.

Aside from the fact that Valerie's penchant for blabbing undermines her productivity as a manager, it also distances her from her staff. They are less likely to ask her questions and share their concerns because they know they'll get caught in a whirlwind of chatter.

While there's nothing wrong with building rapport with your employees and remaining accessible to them, you can waste as much as an hour a day if you babble endlessly rather than express your points succinctly and move on. The most organized managers stick to the topic at hand. By asking questions and making concise statements, they don't hog the spotlight. And they treat each encounter as a chance to learn something from an employee, not as an opportunity to "shoot the breeze."

Another way to improve your organizational skills is to put unsatisfying or aggravating conversations in perspective. You'll sabotage your productivity if you dwell on an argument

Are You an Organized Communicator?

Smart Managing

To test whether you communicate effectively without wasting time, yours and others', monitor how you respond to requests. The next time an employee asks you a question, make sure the first sentence out of your mouth answers it (examples: *yes, no, it depends*). Then use the second sentence to elaborate on your answer, without adding lots of extraneous information. Finally, check whether you kept your entire answer to five sentences or less. That's a desirable goal, because it quickly enables the questioner to follow up or ask for clarification.

and rehash it 20 times in your head. Just because you traded barbs with a smart-mouthed employee doesn't mean you must let it bother you for the rest of the day.

Think of managing as a numbers game. On any given day, you may engage in 25 to 50 separate conversations with employees. Odds are at least one of those interactions will cause at least some problems or leave you angry. If you allow these isolated instances to haunt you or prevent you from focusing on other tasks, then you won't operate at peak efficiency. Remind yourself of all the dialogues that go well, not the few that lead to conflicts.

Conquer "Anticipatory Dread"

New managers must tackle a range of duties that they never had to worry about before. Examples include criticizing an employee's poor work, conducting performance reviews, giving presentations at management meetings, and processing mountains of administrative paperwork.

If you're well organized, then you dive right in and get these tasks accomplished with machine-like efficiency. But many managers don't work that way, at least in their first year on the job. Instead, they devote lots of time to dreading their responsibilities or simply complaining about them to whoever will listen. For every 10 minutes of whining, they may invest one minute of actual work. That's a ratio sure to lead to trouble.

Key Term Anticipatory dread The tendency to think ahead to tasks or job responsibilities that you don't like and dwell on your negative feelings. This forward-looking dread often combines elements of pessimism, cynicism, and fear, and it can lead you to distort the actual task and blow it out of proportion.

To avoid "anticipatory dread," you need to replace negative thoughts with at least some encouragement or optimism. Don't keep telling yourself (and confessing to others) that you "hate having to do this" or "can't stand this part of my job." Each time you remind yourself how much you dislike something, you squander precious time and give yourself an excuse to procrastinate.

What's worse, you reinforce how much you dread it by repeatedly acknowledging that dread.

A better approach is to take a broader, more expansive view. Rather than magnify an unpleasant task that awaits you, remind yourself that "This will take only 30 minutes out of my 50-hour week" or "I'm lucky, because this could be a lot worse."

Capitalizing on Down Time

There's nothing wrong with taking a breather when you're in the midst of hard work. But if you find yourself without any pressing duties and it's a slow day, you may give yourself permission to kick back and enjoy it.

Don't get too comfy.

Organized managers never let themselves coast through the easy times. They welcome seasonal lulls in activity or even a 15-minute block of unscheduled time during an otherwise busy week as a chance to regroup, prepare for hectic times ahead, and consider big-picture affairs.

Use your next pocket of down time to set up "start deadlines." These are specific times within which you must get started on an assignment. By listing those to-do projects that you need to address in the coming months and deciding when you must begin to make progress on each of them, you give yourself a road map to stay organized and systematic in your approach.

While you should also set due dates when you must complete projects, start deadlines play an equally important role. The sooner you get under way, the more time you allot to make progress, so you're less affected by pressure or last-minute snafus.

One of the smartest ways to capitalize on down time is to initiate contact

Killing Time

Beware of indulging yourself during temporary lulls. If you surf the Web aimlessly, rearrange piles on your desk, or flip through reading matter without really absorbing it, then you may feel as if you're keeping busy. But in truth, you might as well take a nap! Time-killing activities can prove costly later when you wish you had spent those minutes engaged in planning.

with employees whom you might otherwise ignore. For example, call workers in field offices and ask how they're doing. Let them report on their current slate of activities and the latest news from the front. Begin by telling them how much time you have to chat: "I have 10 minutes before I need to get to a meeting, so I wanted to catch up and find out how it's going."

You might also want to pounce on a slow period as a time to update and revamp your filing systems. Discard all outdated or inactive materials, such as old magazines or industry reports that you've already digested and don't need to save. Delete all unnecessary e-mail that's clogging your in box. Take stray papers and either file them properly and toss them away.

Making Sense of Your Files

TOOLS Here's a procedure to help you organize your workspace better. Choose relevant categories to archive memos, reference material, and other papers you need to save. Avoid overly broad file tabs such as "pending," "background," or "active." Such terms are too general to help you find what you need. Instead, attach more specific names to each folder. Examples: "purchasing contracts," "marketing reports," "employee benefits," and "technical updates." You'll wind up with more files, but they'll each contain less material and thus prove easier to use.

Showcasing Your Organizational Skills

If you've applied every tool mentioned so far in this chapter and you're now the most organized manager at your firm, don't congratulate yourself just yet. Operating at peak efficiency is not enough. You also need to create the unmistakable impression that you're well organized.

When your colleagues, bosses, and employees perceive you as a productive, can-do manager who follows through with dependability and doesn't squander a second, then they will place a higher value on your time. They will put more trust in your judgments and gain confidence in your ability to tackle many challenges at once.

To demonstrate that you possess superb organizational skills, make them easy for all to see. For example, keep your office clean and don't keep visitors waiting while you rifle through papers to find something you want to show them. And if you need to run to a meeting, don't wait to the last minute to grab all the materials you must bring; instead, pack them in your briefcase ahead of time so that you can stroll out of your office while talking with someone—without having to gather items in a frantic rush.

Here are five ways to ensure that others cannot help but notice and admire your excellent organizational skills:

1. **Give updates.** Deliver on your promises. If you say you're going to do something, either do it right away or keep the other person apprised of your progress. Never force people to nag you and ask, "So what's going on with that project you said you'd get done this week?"

2. **Put it in writing.** Always carry a notepad and don't hesitate to jot down reminders or instructions that others give you. Take notes on what people say, to show that you treat it seriously and you want to remember everything. Think how you feel when you dine at a restaurant and the waiter tries to memorize a long order without using a pad. You worry that you'll get the wrong dish or it won't be prepared as you requested. Same goes when coworkers give you lots of data and you don't show that you're doing something—such as taking notes—to retain it all.

3. **Confirm key facts.** When someone gives you specific information—such as the date and time of a meeting, the full name of someone to look up on a business trip, and the timetable for a project—repeat it to confirm accuracy and prove that you've heard and understood it. Organized managers like to nail down specifics rather than settle for ambiguity. They'll take out their day planners and enter appointments right away, showing the other person that they intend to track that commitment and follow through.

4. **Post your whereabouts.** Some managers plant themselves in their office and barely move the whole day. As a result, they're easily accessible. But if your job requires you to attend lots of meetings or move throughout the office or factory floor, then you may want to leave each day's schedule on your office door to help visitors track you down. Encourage them to leave notes or call you if you're off site. Also change your voice mail recording every day and indicate the time when you'll be either in the office or returning messages from the field.

5. **Keep your office tidy.** Don't glamorize sloppiness by allowing big piles of files to accumulate on your desk or the floor. Some professionals, such as lawyers, bank loan officers, or insurance underwriters, tend to let files stack up around their office. But when you become a manager, leaving mountains of pending work can lead others to think you're unable to handle the burdens of the job. They may view you as a disorganized mess, which can influence how they respond to your authority. Avoid clutter, even if you know where everything's kept. Instead, make a "sweep" of your office at least once a day to clear away debris, empty your in box, and file stray papers.

Making Meetings Work

You've probably attended plenty of meetings, but now that you're a manager your presence will take on a whole new meaning. You'll need to anticipate issues that might get raised and come prepared to answer all sorts of tough questions. If you're disorganized, you'll lose credibility and the chance to win over others.

Beware of taking a laissez-faire attitude at meetings. Don't sit back and let colleagues or staffers babble at will. Many teams get bogged down in needless, time-consuming talk because the group leader's poor organizational skills tend to drag down everyone. You need to set the tone by distributing a clear agenda, inviting the right people, and keeping the proceedings on schedule.

To direct a meeting efficiently, keep it on track. Clearly tell the group what questions need addressing and what issues deserve attention. Write a key problem on a flip chart and emphasize that your goal is to leave the room with at least three specific solutions. If someone veers off on a tangent, gesture to the flip chart as a silent

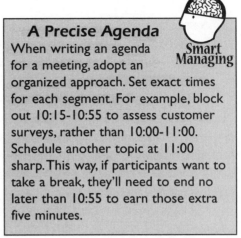

A Precise Agenda

Smart Managing

When writing an agenda for a meeting, adopt an organized approach. Set exact times for each segment. For example, block out 10:15-10:55 to assess customer surveys, rather than 10:00-11:00. Schedule another topic at 11:00 sharp. This way, if participants want to take a break, they'll need to end no later than 10:55 to earn those extra five minutes.

reminder to stick to the core issue. If the speaker continues to ramble, then interrupt by reminding everyone of the time. Say, "Because we only have another 45 minutes, let me jump in and keep us focused on the topic at hand."

If you want to generate buy-in from your staff or show that you listen to their concerns, don't throw the meeting open to general discussion. You may lose control of the proceedings as participants raise concerns that stray too far from the more important priorities you need to cover.

Saving Staff Meetings

When Trish became marketing manager, she continued her predecessor's habit of holding Monday staff meetings. But within a few weeks, she concluded these meetings were time wasters. She tried to impose an agenda, but the group simply used the meetings to complain about various personnel matters. Trish decided to take three steps to improve the situation. First, she met with the most vocal whiners ahead of time so that they wouldn't monopolize the meeting. Second, since the meeting was scheduled to start at 7:45 a.m., she locked the door at exactly 7:50 a.m. so that latecomers wouldn't disrupt the meeting. Third, she arrived early and wrote three words on the flip chart that signified the three most critical topics she wanted the group to discuss. This way, everyone could see where the meeting was heading.

A smarter strategy is to meet privately with influential staffers to let them vent their frustrations or propose their ideas. That way, you can avoid facing runaway meetings where strong-willed individuals attempt to hijack the agenda.

The most effective managers turn meetings into short, productive sessions when decisions get made quickly and employees participate in a collective effort to solve problems. By focusing these gatherings, you can manage your time wisely while modeling for your employees how to stay organized and fight off distractions from all sides.

Manager's Checklist for Chapter 9

❑ Review whether your work habits help you save time, rather than squander it.

❑ Identify the time of the day when you operate at peak productivity, and guard that time so that you can capitalize on it.

❑ When facing big projects, start early and make incremental progress. Don't wait too long to dive in.

❑ Write to-do lists the night before heading to work, rather than once you've arrived at your desk in the morning.

❑ Avoid "anticipatory dread" by not dwelling on how much you don't like to perform certain tasks. Plow ahead without making it harder on yourself.

❑ Run speedy meetings. Distribute a clear agenda, watch the clock, and interrupt babblers to keep everyone on track.

The Right Way to Delegate

"**I**f one more supposed 'expert' tells me I need to do a better job delegating, I'll kill 'em."

I could tell by the way Walt looked at me when he said this that he'd reached his breaking point. A supervisor of a seven-person back-office staff for the last two years, Walt routinely worked 11-hour days. His boss asked me to meet with Walt to make sure the hard-working supervisor didn't burn out.

As soon as I raised the issue of "lightening his load," he shot back, "I've tried everything. There's only so much my employees can do. Believe me, it's not like I insist on doing everything. I'd love it if I could sit back and depend on them more."

The more I spoke with Walt, the clearer the problem became. He assumed he had to do the work himself to get it done properly. His boss held him accountable for producing certain results, and the only way he knew he could deliver was to personally perform those tasks that his staff seemed reluctant, unqualified, or downright unwilling to do.

Without sounding too much like a stuffy consultant, I explained to Walt that his work habits perpetuated a no-win downhill spiral. I helped him realize that his belief that he could do things better than his employees might make him feel good, but it ultimately undermined his ability to manage and advance his career.

An organizational psychologist might diagnose Walt as having *self-enhancement bias*. He inflated his own sense of importance by repeatedly claiming that he had skills, talents, experience, and intuitive ability that far exceeded those of anyone on his staff. As a result, he sighed and said that he "just had to do it all" or else his unit's work would suffer.

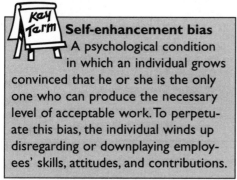

Self-enhancement bias
A psychological condition in which an individual grows convinced that he or she is the only one who can produce the necessary level of acceptable work. To perpetuate this bias, the individual winds up disregarding or downplaying employees' skills, attitudes, and contributions.

Evidence of self-enhancement bias surfaces every day in workplaces everywhere. For example, most new managers readily admit that they're more qualified to do their employees' work than the employees. A recently promoted file clerk will have more confidence in her own filing than in the accuracy of her employees' work. A new personnel manager will trust his instincts on whom to hire more than the judgments of screening interviewers. An accounting manager will spend an extra 30 minutes reviewing his staff's number-crunching because "I trust my work 100%, but not theirs."

This explains why delegating poses such a challenge for so many supervisors, especially rookie managers who're used to doing the work themselves rather than having to oversee others' efforts. If you believe that there's a correlation between the amount of control you exert over a project and the quality of the results, then you'll want to micromanage everything.

Loosening Your Grip

As a new manager, you must accept one hard fact: you can't do it all.

Your success depends on the contributions of your employees. If they grow and continually sharpen their skills, then they'll not only become more valuable assets but also perform their work with more enthusiasm, curiosity, and confidence.

Sounds great, doesn't it? All you have to do is lay off and let them make headway on their own. Resist the urge to step in to finish what they start. Realize that even though you need to wait another 10 minutes for someone to complete a task that you could've breezed through, those 10 minutes are a wise investment in the future. You'll save dozens of hours over the long run by giving employees enough time to grapple with tasks and gain the experience they need to improve.

If you find it hard to loosen your grip, consider the worst-case scenario if you delegate and things go awry. Errors can occur, but you can fix them. And there'll even be an up side: employees who make mistakes and learn from them become more valuable to you, because they now know what *not* to do. Their experience becomes the greatest teacher of all.

Another obstacle to delegating involves time. Some new managers prefer to perform the work themselves because it's quicker to do it than to explain to

> ### Delegate in Steps
> **TRICKS OF THE TRADE**
>
> Force yourself to release the reins a bit by reviewing your to-do list for the day and turning over one entire task to an employee. For example, you could have a staffer make five customer-satisfaction calls or represent you and take notes in an informational meeting. When you delegate, set a time for the two of you to review how it went. Now here's the tough part: forget about it until your follow-up meeting. Don't interfere by hovering over the employee's neck or finding excuses to "drop by" while the work's getting done.

someone else how to do it. That's the rationalization I hear most often when new managers refuse to delegate. My favorite reply is "So you've calculated how much time you'll save over the next six months? The next year?"

It *can* save time to do a job yourself rather than teach an employee. Once. But by the second, third, or fourth time you do it, you'll start to pay the price in time.

Say you insist on checking certain equipment every week, even though your crew is perfectly capable of learning how to conduct competent inspections, because you dread having to explain all the steps to the process, so you do it yourself.

But let's do the math here. You figure it'll take about one hour to give your employees an overview of what to look for during inspections. Then you estimate another two hours per week for the first four weeks, as you review their work and remind them how to do it right. Within a month's time, you can pull back and let them take over completely, because you'll be satisfied they know what they're doing. At that point, you'll gain about an hour a week by not having to do the inspections yourself.

Over the next year, you would thus free up about 48 hours of your time—the equivalent of six full workdays—by investing a total of nine hours in the first month showing employees how to manage this task. If you take the long view, it becomes clear just how much time you'll save by delegating.

Don't assume that as a manager you must take a hands-on interest in each and every assignment. It's more important to spread responsibility among the members of your team and hold them accountable for exercising it. Gen. Colin Powell tells interviewers that a big part of his success as a leader comes from effective delegation. "I have a wide zone of indifference," he likes to say. This helps him give his troops great latitude to make decisions.

Giving Good Directions

Once you realize the long-term benefits of delegating, the next step is to communicate what you need your employees to do in a clear, effective manner. The way that you delegate will largely determine whether your employees respond well and catch on fast.

New managers may have little practice giving instructions. They may wind up repeating themselves, talking down to workers, or assuming too much when explaining what has to get done. Such pitfalls can turn delegating into a disaster.

Here are five of the most common mistakes that rookie managers make when trying to delegate:

1. They "rush and run." To give directions clearly, don't delegate as an afterthought when you're heading off to a meeting. By speaking quickly and then scurrying away, you risk leaving your employees befuddled and uncertain how to proceed. Remember: many workers need extra time to process instructions and gain confidence that they understand how to follow them. If you deny them the opportunity to absorb what you say and ask questions, then you increase the odds of a misfire when they take over. What's worse, they may feel slighted by your hurried attempt to bark orders as you leave the room for something more "important."

2. They improvise poorly. If you're not sure of what you want someone to do, don't think out loud while trying to give instructions. Address your uncertainties ahead of time so that when you delegate, you can spell out exactly what must get accomplished and the best way for the employee to do it. If you leave too much ambiguity, you force others to guess what you mean. That almost guarantees problems in execution.

3. They overexplain. A surefire way to make employees feel dumb is to treat them like children. Don't delegate with the assumption that they're too slow or stupid to understand simple directions. If you needlessly repeat obvious points or speak in a condescending tone, you can alienate your staff. They may spend more energy resenting your communication style than listening to the content of your message.

4. They forget to ask for a demo. Experienced managers learn that some employees may not want to admit that they don't understand something. Instead of saying, "I didn't catch that" or "I'm not sure what you

Repeat After Me

To improve your direction-giving skills, don't repeat your instructions as you give them. You may think you're merely reinforcing key points, but this will make your employees feel like children. Instead, state your directions once and then ask, "Why don't you go over that with me?" or "Will you walk me through how you're going to do this so that we're both assured that I explained this well?"

Smart Managing

mean," they may nod and pretend everything's fine. Don't let that happen. When you delegate, ask employees to demonstrate what you want them to do. Give feedback, offer advice, and praise their progress so that they gain confidence in their skills.

5. They dwell on deadlines. You don't often have the luxury of saying, "Get this done at your leisure." In most cases, you must give the employee a date by which the work must be completed. Yet if you focus too much on the deadline, you may encourage the worker to procrastinate. After all, if you repeat and stress that "this project is due three months from today," that can sound like an eternity to an employee who's barely able to keep pace with his or her daily duties. *It's smarter to set a date by which the staffer must begin the work.* For example, say, "This job's due on October 1. It's now August 5. Can you give me a timetable of when you'll start the research, begin writing your report, and put together your final draft?"

The key to giving good directions is investing the time to communicate effectively. I knew a manager who delegated tasks by jotting a few hurried to-do notes and taping them on an employee's computer monitor. The worker would arrive at his desk in the morning and immediately howl at the prospect of having to decipher these vague, cryptic instructions. Because the manager was almost always in meetings or out of the office, the employee couldn't ask questions to clarify the notes.

Treat delegating as a chance to build rapport with your employees. Chat with them about what needs to get done, how they intend to do it, and why it's important. That may mean spending 10 minutes rather than two minutes assigning a task, but the extra effort up front will surely pay off.

Choosing with Care

Most new managers know it's wise to delegate. After overcoming their inclination to do the work themselves, they realize it's in everyone's interest for them to spread the work around among the members of their team. But they often overlook an important aspect of delegating: choosing the right employee.

Every worker brings strengths and weaknesses to the job. A secretary may possess engaging people skills, but dread reading thick reports. An accountant may crunch numbers well, but fear negotiating with vendors. A salesperson may do excellent market research to identify promising prospects, but lack the perseverance to follow through and contact them.

You must select the best individual for the assignment. The No. 1 delegation problem for new managers is to assume that a job is simple, so anyone can do it. As a result, they pluck an employee at random and say, "Here's what I need done. Get to it." That's a recipe for disaster.

When you delegate, weigh whether you want to discuss the best way for the employee to proceed or just say, "Do this by Friday" and leave it at that. If you want to engage in a true dialogue and hear how the worker intends to follow through, then you want to choose someone who thinks independently and will speak up and share ideas openly with you. But for simple, straightforward tasks, you may not need to discuss ideas or hash out a strategy for implementation.

> **Don't Play Favorites**
> You like and trust certain employees. Perhaps you used to work alongside a few of them and you know they're reliable and competent. So when you decide to delegate, you instantly turn to them. Problem is, if you only ask your "best" workers to help, then you waste the energy and potential of the rest of your crew. You may never learn if they can deliver even better results. And when you put a worker to the test by delegating a critical assignment, you boost that person's confidence.

After a few weeks as a manager, you can probably guess who among your staff will complain, resist, or challenge you when you ask them to do something. If you conclude that you're not going to bother delegating to these stubborn or strong-willed employees, then you'll wind up forcing the more obliging people to bear a heavier load. The result: they may eventually either turn into malcontents or burn out.

Mix and match when you delegate. Reserve time to "sell" at least some jobs to hard-headed or independent-minded employees. Prepare to debate with them the merits of different methods or approaches. Listen with an open mind to their proposals to streamline the task. Welcome their input and praise them for suggesting sensible alternatives.

Rate the Players

TOOLS To make sure you hand off assignments to everyone on your team, rate your employees on a 1-to-10 scale based on how they respond to delegation, with 1 for the most quiet and pliant and 10 for the most stubborn or resistant. Then create a system so that for every easygoing employee (rated 5 or below) to whom you delegate, you force yourself to assign projects to a more demanding staffer (rated 6 or higher). That way, you won't neglect to involve your more difficult employees—thus helping them develop their attitude and expand their skills.

Ideally, you should delegate to employees who are motivated to follow through. Asking an extremely shy technician to substitute for you on a conference panel and give a speech might prove too much for that person. But if you ask that same technician to prepare written "talking points" and then assign a more vocal, less bashful employee to use those points as the basis for the speech, then you can harness the strengths of each individual.

As you get to know your employees, ask them what types of jobs they enjoy the most. Dig to discover their hidden interests or latent talents that you can tap. For example, a customer-service representative who handles phone inquiries may yearn to visit customers face to face. She might make a good candidate to help facilitate a focus group you're establishing. But unless you asked her, you would never know of her eagerness to interact with clients in person.

One way to learn about the kind of duties your employees like is to give each of them a sheet of paper and ask them to write their "wish list" of activities that they're interested in pursuing. They may list interests such as contributing to cross-departmental project teams, getting a chance to control a budget, or gaining exposure to cutting-edge technology.

Armed with this list, you can delegate certain jobs to workers who will pounce on them enthusiastically. This takes much of the guesswork out of determining who should do what among your staff.

Managing a Breakdown

The main reason managers dread delegating is that they fear the work just won't get done. They can wind up having to scoop up the mess left by employees who either didn't understand or didn't remember to follow directions.

New managers must accept this harsh truth: some delegation will fail. Misunderstandings will occur. Managers or their employees will overlook details. Workers will lack the resources to follow through. Disruptions can make it impossible for them to deliver the work on time in a satisfactory manner.

But that's no reason to do everything yourself.

"I'd rather delegate work to someone else that gets done correctly 99% of the time, than have me do it right 100% of the time," says Jay Goltz, owner of Artists' Frame Service, a custom framing store in Chicago. With more than 100 employees and three separate businesses to oversee, Goltz has learned to "manage his managers" so that he's free to run his operation without getting bogged down in minutiae.

By factoring in the few instances when your delegation will go awry, you can prepare yourself for those occasional breakdowns. Rather than use such sporadic disasters to justify micromanaging your staff, you should simply accept them and learn from them.

Don't Disappear After You Delegate

Once you assign a job to an employee, don't assume you can completely wash your hands of the situation. While you need not hover, you should remain accessible if the individual has any questions along the way. If your employee seeks your guidance, it's better to give clear feedback (e.g., "Don't do it that way. Try this way instead.") than to cast the worker adrift (e.g., "It's entirely your call.").

When breakdowns occur, the cause usually revolves around sloppy communication or poor coordination. Either the manager doesn't explain the task clearly or the employee doesn't have the proper knowledge or tools to perform it effectively.

The way you handle these mishaps will largely determine how your employees respond to your future attempts at delegation. If you explode in anger, they'll hesitate to try new approaches or take calculated risks to improve their results. They may also hide the facts from you and pretend everything's fine, only to let a bad situation get worse.

But if you react with equanimity, you assure employees that even the most costly blunders aren't going to rupture your relationship. Your calm, clear-headed response sends a message that you'd prefer to know the outcome right away—even if it's bad news.

Follow these guidelines when you learn your delegation has backfired:

- **Focus on solutions.** Don't rush to assign blame in the midst of a snafu. After you gather the facts and confirm your understanding of what happened, dwelling on the problem only exacerbates it. Even if it appears obvious that your employee simply dropped the ball, don't judge too soon or express your disappointment too angrily. There'll be time for assessments later and finger-pointing as you see fit. For now, maintain a forward-looking view. Prod your employee to weigh "What next?" questions. Work together to plot the best strategy to salvage the situation.
- **Keep your perspective.** Some new managers aren't used to breakdowns. They may buckle under the pressure and blow their cool. You'll know that you're losing it if you start grumbling, "Why didn't I do this myself?" or "I knew I couldn't trust Bill to handle this." Contain your self-flagellation. Don't beat yourself mercilessly because your attempt at delegation failed. Remind yourself of the worst-case scenario and think of the big picture. This

A Bad Day Just Got Worse

When Stella, a new manager, learned that her secretary had entered the wrong numbers on a financial report to be distributed to the CEO, she blew her stack. Upon hearing the distressing news, her face turned beet-red and she told her secretary, "I trusted you to do this right! It's so simple. I thought, 'This time I won't do this myself. I'll let you do it.' So much for that. That was a stupid idea." Of course, Stella's outburst made her secretary feel worse than ever and didn't accomplish anything. It turns out that Stella was able to intercept the report before it landed on the CEO's desk, so no harm was done. Except that she alienated an otherwise competent employee who had made one careless mistake.

mess may annoy you now but chances are it will have little or no lasting impact.

- **Don't forget to dissect**. Once you recover from the breakdown, wait a few days and analyze it. Strive to learn from your mistakes in delegating the task and your employee's errors in following through. Approach this not as a detective trying to find out who's guilty but as a dispassionate reporter trying to assemble the facts accurately to shed light on how events unfolded. Involve your employee in the process. Politely explain that your goal is to extract lessons from the breakdown so that you can prevent problems in the future.

Bottom-Up Delegation

You may assume that delegation always travels downward, from the boss to the subordinate. Actually, it works best when it arises out of a dialogue between supervisor and staffer, where each person can contribute ideas in order to finalize an action plan that the staffer will carry out.

Ideally, delegation should flow from discussions between managers and staff where the boss describes a goal or challenge and invites workers to help define a solution. Most employees prefer to participate in a joint search for knowledge rather than be spoon-fed exactly what they need to know and

Key Term **Participative delegation** The process of allowing your employees to participate in crafting their own assignments and deciding the best way for them to implement them. This consists of dialogues, such as brainstorming sessions and mutual problem-solving, rather than one-way order-giving.

what they must do as a result. If they're bossed around every step of the way, they will turn into reactive zombies rather than energetic, free-thinking team members.

To ensure that you use participative delegation, get into the habit of telling your employees, "Here's what I need done," and asking two questions: "How would you go about it?" and "What do you see as the pros and cons of that approach?" This trains them to consider the most efficient way to execute a plan, rather than just blindly following your orders.

When employees play a role in shaping their assignment, they buy into it more forcefully. They'll also take ownership of the result.

Why? Because when workers know *why* they're doing something and they help determine *how* they're going to do it, then the odds of success soar. They are fully engaged in the process, which heightens their motivation and increases their concentration.

Here's how to prove it to yourself. Stage a two-prong experiment. First ask an employee to do something—with no questions asked and no discussion. Just give an order, make sure it's understood, and leave it at that. Then try delegating the same task to another employee with a similar level of knowledge and experience. But this time, use participative delegation. Aside from the two questions above, you may want to ask, "What do you think about this?" and "What are your ideas on how to get this done?"

Compare the results. You'll probably find that the task is completed far more effectively by the second employee. Better yet, this employee may provide a value-added bonus: rather than merely figuring out how to attain your goal, he or she may propose additional ideas or uncover new ways to accomplish old tasks.

When you enable employees to help define the nature and scope of their work, they care about it more. And that not only leads to better results, but makes your job as manager much easier.

Manager's Checklist for Chapter 10

❏ You gain more control as a manager by giving it away in the form of delegation. Micromanaging creates limitations.

❏ While you may save time in the short term by doing a job yourself, weigh the long-term costs of neglecting to delegate.

❏ When giving directions, leave time to answer employees' questions and solicit their ideas.

❏ Supply key facts, such as the goal of the project and its deadline. But don't overexplain or provide too much information. This can make employees feel dumb.

❏ Don't play favorites when you delegate. Spread assignments around so that everyone's contributing and you're trying to match the type of work with individual strengths.

❏ If you delegate and the job doesn't get done properly, focus on solutions. Don't overreact or rush to pin blame on your employee.

Managing the Boss

M ark liked his boss. As a star computer programmer for a financial services firm, Mark felt that the best thing his boss could do was "stay out of my way." And Mark's boss happily complied.

But when Mark earned a promotion and became a manager, his boss could no longer leave him alone. Now the stakes were higher. Mark's responsibility didn't end with his own technical ability; his success as manager would depend on the accomplishments of others.

"When I became a manager, my boss suddenly took on a different role," Mark said. "Instead of trusting my judgment and letting me experiment, he would demand lots of information from me every week. He wanted to know what I was doing, what my employees were doing, what we planned to do the coming week, what problems we were having—it was like he had to know everything."

Mark confronted a common challenge that new managers face: how to satisfy the boss.

When you become a manager for the first time, it's natural for your boss to take an increased interest in your job performance. That's because you're moving from an area where you've proven yourself into uncharted terrain.

Upward Communication Dangers

When you talk with your employees, there's always the chance for misunderstanding. You may give vague instructions, offer unclear explanations, or provide ambiguous answers to their questions.

When you talk with your boss, a whole new set of potential pitfalls can derail your communication. You may misinterpret an order as a mere suggestion, or vice versa. Or you may read meaning into a passing comment and assume the boss is trying to drop a subtle hint. Even the boss's jokes can cause anxiety if you think there's a message behind the humor.

When interacting with their boss, new managers often wonder, "What's he trying to tell me?" or "Am I missing something here?" Confusion can result, leaving the hapless manager guessing at what the boss wants.

It's normal to feel a bit insecure at first. No one wants to look dumb and ask a boss, "What are you telling me?" "Can you speak more clearly?" or "Can you translate that into plain English?"

Thus far we've discussed the danger of trying to decipher the boss's remarks. Let's not forget the problems that *you* can create by not speaking clearly. Problems can ensue if you're reluctant to level with your boss, provide specific information, or give bad news.

If your goal is to inform or educate your boss, avoid limiting yourself to general statements. Instead, lace your com-

Clarify Without Fear

Smart Managing

Here's a tactic to cut through the boss's cryptic remarks and unearth the true message. Begin by saying, "Let me ask you a clarifying question." Then repeat something the boss said, verbatim. Close by asking, "Can you expand on that?" or "Is your intent then for me to …?" Some bosses will jump in the moment you repeat what they said, saving you from having to ask them anything. They may volunteer more information or explain their reasoning in more detail. In any case, it's important to parrot back the same words you heard—even if they make no sense to you. If you attempt to paraphrase, you invite more confusion.

ments with facts such as dates, times, statistics, and objective measurements of performance. The benefits are twofold: you show your boss how you've arrived at your conclusion and you demonstrate your command of the kind of quantitative information that bosses can easily relay to *their* bosses.

If you want to win over your boss, then you also want to cite plenty of persuasive evidence to buttress your position. Ideally, you should succinctly summarize what you want your boss to do. Then think in threes (see Chapter 5) so that you give a trio of cogent, hard-hitting reasons why your boss should approve your proposal.

Regardless of whether you're trying to inform or persuade your boss, it's important to avoid making too many groundless claims or assertions without proof. In your effort to showcase your early progress as a manager or to curry favor with your boss, you may wind up exaggerating your team's accomplishments or setting unrealistically high expectations.

While bold, blustery comments can help you come across as a confident leader, such cockiness can come back to haunt you over the long term if your boss loses faith in what you say. As a new manager, preserving and strengthening your credibility should guide your upward communication.

Here are three things to avoid when speaking with your boss:

1. Evasion. In your first few months as a manager, you probably want to minimize the bad news you must deliver to your boss. You also want to avoid too many "I don't know" answers, for fear of appearing ignorant or unprepared. So you wind up playing the evasion game, bobbing and weaving so that you don't have to say anything unpleasant, admit your lack of knowledge, or divulge troubling information about your unit's performance.

Evasion may buy you time, but it doesn't offer much of a solution. Indeed, most bosses will see through your hesitance to answer their questions head-on and volunteer the kind of useful data that can help everyone assess a situation more effectively.

2. The fact-opinion blur. Now that you're a manager, you may think that your opinions suddenly carry more weight. The result: when you chat with your boss, you feel free to let the dogmatic comments fly. You figure that one of the perks of power is not having to substantiate what you say. You can just make predictions and label your staff with impunity, right?

Wrong. Bosses can tell when their supervisors state opinions that are disguised as facts. I call this "the fact-opinion blur." There's nothing wrong with occasionally offering your views, but if you state them as if they're self-evident truths, you risk sounding arrogant. And most bosses hate to manage know-it-alls.

3. Playing telephone. If you're going to serve as your boss's eyes and ears, make sure you're accurate. Alerting your boss of rumors or passing along other tidbits of unconfirmed data can backfire if it turns out that you're mistaken.

Managing your upward communication is like playing "telephone," where each participant whispers a message to the next person. By the time the message travels from the first sender to the last receiver, it has been greatly distorted.

Caught in the Middle

Managing a boss is easy when everything goes well. But during a crisis, tensions can rise as tempers flare. That's when individuals let slip the kind of unfortunate comments that leave lasting scars.

The most difficult situations arise when rookie managers struggle to satisfy angry employees while complying with the boss's controversial orders.

> **Speaking for the Record**   TRICKS OF THE TRADE
>
> Improve your upward communication by inserting lots of "according to" statements. This means attributing a fact or observation to the proper source so that your boss can assess its reliability. Example: "Our retention rate is up 7% year-to-date, according to a report I requested from Ralph Smith in marketing."

I met a foreman at a manufacturing facility who had to decide after only three weeks on the job whether to follow his boss's direction to turn off the air conditioning on the factory floor—or leave it on to make the workplace bearable for his laborers.

Looking worried and worn, he called it a "lose-lose deal." If he obeyed his boss's command to shut off the air conditioning, his employees would surely rebel (or simply quit). If he ignored the order, he risked punishment for insubordination.

He couldn't decide what to do. Finally, when his boss asked how the workers had responded to the lack of air conditioning, the beleaguered foreman blurted out, "The real question is why they don't walk out of this hellhole? I ask myself the same thing sometimes." Naturally, the boss blew up at the foreman's snide remark. Their relationship only worsened after that, until the foreman agreed to resign a few months later.

What the foreman should have done—aside from controlling his emotions and unleashing his frustrations in a more productive manner—is to ask his boss the reasons for the order. Had he done so, he would have learned that his boss was under extreme pressure from the president to cut costs. Armed with this insight, the foreman could have proposed other measures to reduce operating expenses and even relayed some sensible money-saving suggestions that his crew had mentioned to him.

Even if he couldn't come up with any better ideas to cut costs, asking his boss for the rationale for such an unpopular move would at least have helped him explain it to his employees. Instead, he was left shrugging and rolling his eyes when his furi-

---

TOOLS

The Manager as Conduit

When you pass along an order from your boss that you know will trigger an outcry from the troops, follow this three-step procedure. First, explain the order in clear, neutral language. Don't reveal contempt for the boss or otherwise criticize or mock the boss. Second, reinforce a larger goal, such as the organization's need to survive a business downturn or the importance of making collective sacrifices to facilitate teamwork and increase long-term job security for everyone. Finally, reserve time for questions. Don't just tell workers what they must do; let them vent and listen patiently to their concerns.

ous workers demanded to know why "the bigwigs at this place don't want us to have air conditioning."

In many cases, it's wise to tell a boss that you disagree with an order. But don't magnify the situation by pretending it's a life-or-death matter. Use phrases such as "Another strategy that strikes me as more appealing is ..." or "As much as I disagree with that, I understand what you're trying to do." Speak in a pleasant tone; don't overdramatize your remarks. Conclude by reassuring your boss that, despite your misgivings, you will comply with the instruction to the best of your ability. (Of course, if you're asked to break a rule or behave unethically, you're justified in refusing to comply.)

At some point, almost every new manager gets caught in the middle. You're not alone. Treat this as just another aspect of the job that you need to manage, not as a drop-dead crisis. Realize that every boss looks like an idiot or makes unreasonable demands on occasion, and you must choose the most appropriate, professional response.

Pick the Right Personality

Just be yourself.

That's fine advice if you're on a first date, trying to hit it off and make sparks fly. But to manage your boss, your personality could work against you. It depends on the type of person the boss likes most. Some executives love to boss around relatively helpless worrywarts who're meek and compliant. Others prefer to cultivate free-thinking leaders who don't need much direction. In any case, you may need to adapt your personality to appeal more effectively to your boss.

Of course, if your boss wants someone who is meek and compliant, that's not a boss you want to use as a role model. Understand what you need to do to interact effectively with your manager, but don't be afraid to assert yourself when you have useful information or an idea to share. Do this with diplomacy and tact, but do it. Otherwise, you'll be unhappy and won't be adding much value to the organization. Such bosses, by the way, often don't survive. So if you have one like that, be patient.

New managers may exhibit one of four personality traits. A mismatch between your personality and your boss's means there is a real possibility of conflict between the two of you.

Denyers turn away from unpleasantness. They deny any harsh reality. They figure, "If I don't think about it, it'll go away on its own." These managers may withhold their concerns from their boss or sugarcoat a serious problem because they just don't have the stomach to confront it head-on. What's worse, they may convince themselves over time that no problems exist.

If you're a denyer, then you'd better hope you have an equally oblivious boss. If both of you agree to disregard certain issues or simply pretend that everything's fine, then you can proceed without fear of punishment. Crises won't disappear, of course, but at least you'll have the support from above to manage them by ignoring them.

> **⚠️ CAUTION!**
> ### Hiding the Truth
> In the early months of establishing a relationship with a new boss, beware of denying or brushing away potential problems. You may prefer to compartmentalize and block off certain areas, but the boss may misinterpret your refusal to deal with certain issues as a stubbornness or weakness to fix what's broken. Listen to your boss's concerns and acknowledge them. Raise some of your own, too. Show that you're willing to analyze even the thorniest parts of your job dispassionately and hash out solutions.

Jokesters use humor as their favorite coping mechanism. Even if they're in over their heads, they crack jokes and keep smiling. They may resort to harmless puns, good-natured riddles, or even minor pranks to dispel tension around the office. Or they may regale listeners (including their bosses) with long stories that deliver only questionably funny punch lines.

Some rookie managers resort to gallows humor to describe their experience. I've heard newly minted managers refer to themselves as "prisoners of war" or "Death Row inmates" because they feel trapped in a position that offers no peace or escape. While some bosses may find such talk offensive, such as an executive who's a Vietnam veteran and knows firsthand what it's like fighting a war, others may indulge a jokester and even try to top the new manager by volleying back with more witticisms.

If you use humor to cover certain insecurities, make sure your boss appreciates—or at least tolerates—your behavior. Watch how he or she acts when you say something you think adds humor to the situation. If you're greeted with a blank face or even a dash of annoyance or impatience, that's a sure sign you should cut the mirth and focus more intently on serious matters. Recognize as well that if you're using humor to mask certain inadequacies in your skills or lack of information, you need to address these inadequacies directly. Get training. Do your homework so you can speak with authority. Then you can use humor good-naturedly and not to mask a problem. *Worriers* always seem discouraged or overwhelmed. And most bosses dread having to manage them.

Cutting the Wisecracks

Jan loved to joke around. When she became a manager, she figured her brand of humor would endear her to her staff and her boss, Karen. While her employees liked her witty nature, Karen viewed her as a "lightweight." Karen thought that Jan's constant need to crack jokes was a weakness, indicating that she couldn't take things seriously. What's more, Karen rarely laughed. Jan realized she needed to adjust her personality to build a better rapport with Karen, so she made an effort to mimic Karen's communication style: straightforward, precise, and humorless. Karen began to like and trust Jan, and Jan eventually loosened up again—but only when she could use her humor to provide a welcome relief.

If you tend to fret over every decision or habitually talk about your ever-mounting anxieties, then consider the effect that has on your boss. You'll hardly build your boss's confidence in your management; in fact, you may needlessly undermine your image by coming across as a sky-is-falling pessimist.

Ironically, many worriers are actually competent managers. Their fretful nature may disguise their steely determination to tackle multiple tasks well. But their bosses may conclude that these managers simply lack the poise and inner strength to persevere during tough times.

"I've got a new manager who pushes the panic button every day," a vice president of human resources told me. "She is always on edge, worrying about stuff that doesn't merit even a second of thought. It's too bad, because it really limits her effectiveness."

If you're a worrier, then it will almost definitely work against you if you want to build rapport with your boss. Unless you're "lucky" enough to report to someone who's also a stress-monger—in which case the two of you may work yourselves into a tizzy together—then you're better off venting your anxieties outside of work in a safe manner. Help your boss see you as a strong, sturdy manager who won't crumble under pressure.

Impulsives have short attention spans. They will talk without thinking, thus resulting in frequent bouts of foot-in-mouth disease. They also wind up putting out fires all day, because they do not plan or take preventive steps to avoid blowups down the line.

Some bosses enjoy managing impulsives for their shoot-from-the-hip honesty. But if you're a new manager with an impulsive personality, don't count on having a receptive boss. If you're easily daunted by the prospect of plotting a strategy and then implementing it slowly in stages, then you may drive your higher-ups crazy.

Many bosses conclude that impulsives are actually lazy. They may figure that if you don't like to think through what you're going to do before you plunge in, then you're simply undisciplined, disorganized, or both. You won't stand a chance of getting ahead if you continue to act impulsively with a disapproving boss.

Instead, force yourself to explain how you're going to tackle a project. Get into the habit of breaking an assignment into numbered steps—and then telling your boss what how you've designed a "three-step process" or a "two-prong attack to this problem." This shows that you're not jumping right into a task and it proves you're able to control your impulsiveness when it counts.

Remember, we all have our personality quirks. We need to be tolerant of one another and focus on strengths and abilities—our own, those of our employees, and those of our managers. We also need to focus on improving our ability to add value and to communicate honestly, even when the news is not good. This usually works best to promote compatible working relationships.

> **Smart Managing**
>
> ### Follow a "Two-Second Clock"
>
> If you tend to blurt out whatever's on your mind, you may let slip comments that your boss finds silly, insulting, or simply incorrect. You need to tame your impulsive side.
>
> Here's how. When talking with your boss, mentally count to two before you speak. This applies whether you're responding to a question or making a statement. Then, after completing your point, stop talking. Some impulsives will add to what they've just said with spontaneous asides that prove needless and distracting.

The Magic of "Underpromise/Overdeliver"

The best way to manage your boss is to manage your boss's expectations. By consistently producing *more* work and *better* results than your boss has any reason to anticipate, you'll stand out as an exceptional new manager.

The trick to setting the right expectations involves two steps. First, initiate projects that'll have a direct bottom-line impact. Then define how you'll track your progress. Don't wait for your superiors to tell you what to do, or you'll have to measure up to whatever standards they've set for your success.

Say you want to enact reforms to increase the responsiveness of your firm's customer service. You write a three-part memo to your boss outlining your goal, an action plan to meet it, and a timetable for producing results. But don't commit to stretch goals in writing. Make sure to set realistic objectives that you're sure you can meet—and exceed. That way, you leave your boss even more impressed with your performance.

Same goes when you're discussing a project face to face with your boss. Resist the urge to commit to something you're not absolutely sure you can deliver. It's better to set the bar lower at the outset and raise it as you go along.

In weighing what kind of goals you should set, consider your boss's frame of reference. The only way to ensure that you underpromise and overdeliver is if you take the time to understand how your boss perceives the situation. Ask yourself these questions first:

- "How is my boss held accountable by his bosses? What measurements do they use to evaluate his success?"
- "What pressures does my boss face?"
- "How does my boss track my work performance?"
- "What does my boss expect from me? What would it take for me to exceed those expectations?"
- "To what extent will my boss notice or care if I exceed expectations? What steps can I take to call attention to my results?"

If your boss pushes you beyond your limits and sets absurdly high expectations, then underpromising and overdelivering may seem impossible. But it's not. That's because you should not accept the boss's goals blindly. Instead, explain the basis for your more realistic expectations. Then add, "I like the challenge you've laid out. I'm not going to promise you what I can't deliver, but I can promise you'll get 100% from me all the time." That way, you set the stage to delight your boss by proving you can push yourself further than you thought you could go.

Giving Progress Reports

Bosses love information.

The more you can furnish them with the latest numbers—from weekly sales and expenses to historical trends (such as month-to-month results)—the more comfortable they'll feel both in assessing your performance and in relaying the numbers to their higher-ups. By tracking the same hard data as the boss, you also prove that you're thinking like the boss. That builds your credibility.

Soon after you become a manager, ask your boss what key ratios or benchmarks matter most in your unit. Confirm how you can compute these numbers accurately and make sure you have access to the necessary information. For example, a new underwriting manager at an insurance company may be held accountable for maintaining a low "loss ratio." (This is how insurance executives calculate how much money the company collects versus the amount paid in claims to its policyholders.) A manager would want to arrange for daily updates on loss ratio to avoid surprises—and angry bosses bursting in and demanding answers for poor results.

Invite your boss to tell you the best way to communicate your unit's performance. Don't assume that just because you like to chat face to face, so does your manager. Most executives prefer memos or financial reports, along with graphs, charts, and tables. Others may want to monitor your work online through an intranet or request spreadsheets they can download directly from your computer. Periodically check to confirm that you're supplying your boss with the right information in the best format.

> **A Menu of Choices** Tricks of the Trade
>
> Manage your boss more effectively by listing all the gauges you use to measure your unit's performance. Examples might include sales per employee, turnover rate, customer complaints, budgeting and payroll, etc. Then ask your boss to rank all the measures in order of importance or relevance for assessing you and your team. Armed with this information, you ensure that your progress reports will serve a valuable purpose in giving the boss exactly what he or she needs.

While it's tempting to underscore your victories when giving updates to higher-ups, the real test of your boss-management skills comes when you must acknowledge poor results or admit errors. It's understandable to show reluctance in confessing missed targets, blown opportunities, or careless blunders. But that's no excuse to bury the bad news.

New managers may try to let slip the disappointing news in between lots of "happy talk." That's usually a mistake. Nothing irritates a boss more than having someone introduce a gloomy note into an otherwise upbeat conversation. It's better to wait for a moment when you're both in neutral business mode, reviewing the organization's goals and analyzing the latest numbers. That way, you can tie your message to bottom-line concerns and present a solution that'll make the bad news easier to swallow.

> **⚠ CAUTION!**
> **Manipulating Results**
> Some managers, whether they are new or not, have a tendency to manipulate the numbers to meet some established goal or target. It's almost always possible to make the numbers look better. For example, you can put off posting costs to the next month or you can include future expected sales in a current month's report. Resist the temptation to do this. It will catch up with you, and it takes your focus away from what you should be doing—learning from your experience and taking actions to improve the performance of your group and the organization.

Show a willingness to take responsibility for setbacks, even if you're not personally at fault. Most bosses appreciate having an honest, straightforward manager who doesn't shift blame when problems erupt. When you say, "This happened on my watch, so I take responsibility," chances are your boss will insist that you not take it so hard. And that's exactly the kind of relationship you want to establish.

Manager's Checklist for Chapter 11

❑ When communicating with your boss, avoid groundless claims or assertions without proof. Instead, amass plenty of facts to support your position.

❑ Beware of stating your opinions as facts. Bosses often see through this and it can raise their suspicions.

❑ When relaying your boss's unpopular orders to your staff, explain them in clear, neutral language. Then reinforce a larger, organizational goal and leave time for questions.

❑ If you disagree with your boss, do so without overdramatizing it. Simply point out how your view differs and provide evidence to support your position.

❏ Don't boast to your boss about how you intend to exceed even the most ambitious performance goals. Instead, underpromise and overdeliver.

❏ Learn how your boss prefers to absorb information and review your progress. Identify the key ratios or numbers that drive your unit's performance and then track the same data.

Cultivating a Network

It's lonely at the top. At least that's what some fast-rising managers say when they no longer can open up with their coworkers.

Now that they wield authority, they have to watch what they say and cut their griping. They're often left isolated from people that they can trust, especially when they're not comfortable chatting with their boss.

Yet it doesn't have to come to this. You can ascend into management ranks without severing all ties with your former coworkers. And with some aggressive networking, you can use your new job to open doors that provide access to a whole new cast of high-powered characters.

To expand your circle of corporate friends and acquaintances, it's important to sharpen your professional presence. If you radiate confidence, you'll draw people to you. But if you appear anxious, forlorn, or constantly distracted, others will steer clear of engaging in conversation with you.

Establishing a professional presence involves a complex set of variables. You want to attract just the right amount of positive attention, like an intriguing and appealing package in a store— without going overboard. And you want to put people at ease.

Don't get caught up in trivia. How you dress does not really matter as much as how you express yourself. As long as you aren't decked out in glaringly inappropriate clothing, then the fact that your pants are a quarter-inch too long or you have a slight stain on your shirt collar won't matter. Yet your facial expression, posture, and willingness to launch conversa-

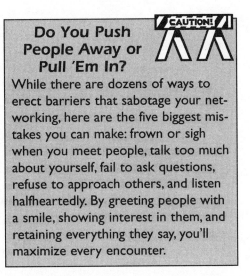

Do You Push People Away or Pull 'Em In?

While there are dozens of ways to erect barriers that sabotage your networking, here are the five biggest mistakes you can make: frown or sigh when you meet people, talk too much about yourself, fail to ask questions, refuse to approach others, and listen halfheartedly. By greeting people with a smile, showing interest in them, and retaining everything they say, you'll maximize every encounter.

tions *do* matter. You need to make others believe you enjoy talking with them. By welcoming opportunities to meet and greet people—rather than avoiding them—you'll become a much more productive and formidable networker.

Make the First Minute Count

You don't need to attend conferences or trade group meetings to network. As a new manager, you have a perfect opportunity to introduce yourself to colleagues throughout your organization. And the more contacts you can forge at your company, the greater your chances of making friends in high places, monitoring the rumor mill, and learning about functions or departments other than your own.

It all begins with a pleasant greeting and an outstretched hand. Turning to a stranger in the elevator and saying, "Hi, I'm Chris Jones" can only work to your advantage. At best, you can get to know someone who will make your new management job easier. At worst, your five-second investment of time will not pay off as the conversation sputters to a halt. Even then, however, there's no harm done.

Soon after striking up a conversation, you may find yourself fighting off a host of nagging irritants. For instance, if your initial

Opening Lines

TRICKS OF THE TRADE   To ease into conversations with strangers, prepare a few all-purpose icebreakers. Before saying "Hello, I'm …," you may prefer to preface your remarks with a friendly comment such as "I should introduce myself." Once you get past the introduction, be ready to carry the dialogue forward: "I'm a new manager in the _____ department." Explaining your role almost guarantees that the other person will say something at least somewhat interesting or relevant to you. Another example: "I notice that you're carrying/wearing/working on …." Using your observational skills to spark a more lively, personal exchange can work well if you want to learn more about someone.

judgment of the other person is negative, that may cloud your ability to listen with an open mind. This can happen as soon as you hear someone's voice, which may have an accent you dislike or a cold, stern tone you find objectionable. Or you may find yourself trapped with a motor mouth who monopolizes your time as you seek an escape. What's worse, you may grow so self-conscious that you neglect to pay attention. Any traces of insecurity can intensify if you sense that the other person finds you somehow off-putting.

To test whether you're in the right frame of mind to network successfully, monitor your thoughts as the conversation begins. Ideally, you should focus on the three following points:

- Learn more.
- Make the other person feel comfortable.
- Express genuine enthusiasm for the chance to get to know each other.

On the other hand, if your mind wanders and encounters any of these thoughts, you're already digging yourself into a hole:

- I look terrible today.
- I'm not in the mood to continue this.
- I don't like this person.

The surest way to sabotage your networking is to prejudge others. Based on someone's attitude or appearance, you may figure it's not worth the effort to introduce yourself. Or perhaps

A New Beginning

When Warren became a manager, he decided that he needed to expand his network throughout the five-floor corporate headquarters where he worked. So whenever he saw a familiar
face in the hallway, parking lot or cafeteria, he'd say, "I've seen you
around. I want to introduce myself. I'm Warren, and I just started as a
manager in the electronics unit." In some cases, people didn't warm up
right away. They gave a perfunctory response that hurt Warren's feelings. But he persevered, doing this so many times that it became auto-
matic. After approaching 10 or so people, he no longer took it personally if they didn't seem friendly. He just kept them talking until they
could establish at least some rapport.

you've heard damning statements about this person through the
grapevine, so you avoid as much as a simple "hello."

Even if you rise above these concerns and try to chat, you
may not treat certain individuals as openly if you perceive them
as tainted. Banish all negative judgments from your mind when
you launch a conversation.

Radiate enthusiasm with your body language when you first
meet someone. Give a firm handshake while standing up
straight with your weight balanced evenly on both feet. Don't tilt
your head to one side or start talking with downcast eyes. Look
directly at the person. Try to communicate warmth and good
will with pleasant facial expressions and open, welcoming gestures. The best networkers put people at ease from the outset,
and that makes the conversation flow more smoothly.

Tracking Your Progress

As you're probably discovering, almost every aspect of managing involves the use of systems, processes, and record keeping.
Many new managers find that they've never before kept track of
so much information—or had so many ways to analyze it.

Same goes with networking. If you want to make more contacts and ensure that you're "in the loop," you can't leave it to
chance or allow your mood to dictate when you feel like meeting new people. Instead, set a goal of establishing a set number
of new acquaintances every week. In making contacts, you

may even want to distinguish between people inside and outside your organization.

For example, say you decide you want to add at least five individuals to your network every week. You work at a small company, so networking internally isn't necessary. That means you need to seek out new faces by asking yourself, "Who do I want to get to know?" You conclude it's best to befriend customers, vendors, suppliers, and even some managers who work at rival firms.

The next step is to log your results. You keep a notebook to tally every networking encounter. An easy way to do this is to divide the page into three columns with the headings "who," "topics discussed," and "commitments." Then, in the moments after you part ways with someone you've just met, you can fill in the blanks in your notebook.

You may think it's strange or inappropriate to keep such formal records of your informal chats. But it serves a purpose. By counting your contacts and recording what others tell you, you hold yourself more accountable. If you set a goal of adding five people to your notebook every week, then you will know at a glance how you're doing. And your fleeting mood swings or fears of rejection or embarrassment won't stop you if you're determined to reach your weekly objective.

Capture Those Details!

Smart Managing   When tracking your networking, pay special attention to recording the "topics discussed." Rather than describe the conversation in vague terms such as "talked shop" or "compared notes," be specific. For example, write "analyzed disaster recovery plans" or "shared new product rollout experiences." Also confirm the spelling of the person's full name in the "who" column, ideally by getting a business card. Finally, when you tell someone you'll "try" to do something rather than promise to do it, you may still want to jot that down in the "commitments" column. This will prod you to follow through.

In some cases, you can get out your notebook during the conversation. If the speaker gives you his phone number, recommends a book, or suggests checking out a certain Web site, reach for pen and pad and say, "Give me a moment. I want to write this down." The benefit is twofold: the speaker will appreciate that you clearly intend to follow up and you won't have to risk forgetting these facts later by waiting to write them down.

If you want to learn even more from your record keeping, then chart your week-to-week progress. Every Friday afternoon, count the number of contacts you've made. Then graph the results in your notebook or on your computer screen. Within a few months, you'll begin to easily spot any dips or surges in your networking activity. This can help you identify the challenges that can block your outreach efforts, such as falling behind during the last week of every month when you're facing deadlines. Armed with this awareness, you can take steps to maintain your networking pace despite such obstacles.

Who Knows About You?

You're now a manager, but that doesn't mean everyone throughout your organization knows about it. When you walk down the hall, there's no sign around your neck that reads "I was just promoted to manager!" Unless you're suddenly dressing differently or you now have an office in the executive suite, casual observers may have no way of understanding your new role. It's up to you to spread the word—without overdoing it.

If your boss sends out a memo announcing your promotion, don't assume everyone will read it. Many new managers tell me they're dispirited by how few people know or care about their happy news. "They just don't read this mail" or "It's like things haven't changed" are common complaints.

But you need not rely on your boss or the folks in Human Resources to compose a snappy memo to alert your colleagues about your promotion. You can toot your own horn—and network successfully at the same time. Here are three ways to do it:

1. **Query your company.** Some authors will send a note to the editor of the Sunday book review section of their newspaper with a request seeking information on an obscure topic. The authors hope the editor runs the letter in the newspaper, thus turning thousands of readers into

potential research assistants. You can borrow this tactic to make contacts in your organization. Send a company-wide e-mail explaining a project you're working on and asking for help, such as seeking volunteers for a cross-departmental team. In the memo, mention your new position as manager and the project's benefits to the firm. This is a relatively painless way to network, because respondents will ultimately come to you. And your coworkers can become valuable sources of information to help you do your job better. Note: You may need permission from higher-ups before sending company-wide e-mail, so check whether you need to get the proper approvals first.

2. **Make the rounds.** Contact department heads and offer to serve as guest speaker at their staff meetings. Also invite colleagues in other parts of the firm to luncheons or award ceremonies with your employees. The more you break down barriers among units of your organization, the easier you can mingle with people in other departments.

3. **Join cross-departmental teams.** One of the easiest ways to network is to get yourself named to groups that collaborate on big projects. By contributing your expertise to the team, you can earn the respect of influential executives whom you would never otherwise meet.

When you attend company events, such as a picnic or a training seminar, don't cling to coworkers. Strike up conversations with the person sitting next to you in class or standing behind you in line in the cafeteria. Even if you just commiserate together about the bad weather or discuss the exploits of your local sports teams, that's enough to get you started. The next time you see that person, you can build on that contact.

Fighting Off Fears

Let me guess: you're buried in work, trying to make sense of your new job as manager. You know it's a good idea to network, but you just don't have the time.

That's no excuse.

Meeting people both inside and outside your organization is imperative to your career advancement. Plus, you never know what you'll learn by initiating contact with a variety of professionals.

Even if you see the value of networking, you may conclude you're just too anxious or scared. Fear can let you off the hook.

Unless you're a natural extrovert, you may prefer to keep a low profile and limit your small talk with strangers. That's the easy way out—but it comes at a price: you'll limit your effectiveness as a manager and you'll isolate yourself and lack allies when you need them.

If the thought of introducing yourself to people rattles you, then conquer your fears. You need to move outside of your comfort zone so that you take risks and increase the number of "cold chats" that you initiate. The more conversations you launch with people you don't know, the more doors will open for you and the more insights you'll collect to improve how you manage.

If you're reluctant to network more aggressively, even though you know it's a wise idea, you're probably succumbing to some mild if not severe fears. Once you expose these

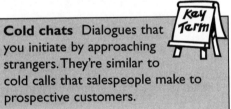

Cold chats Dialogues that you initiate by approaching strangers. They're similar to cold calls that salespeople make to prospective customers.

anxieties and develop strategies to overcome them, you can proceed with more confidence.

Here are three of the most common fears that may inhibit you:

1. Fear of embarrassment. When starting a conversation with someone you don't know, your mind can play tricks on you. Rather than enjoying the moment, you may convince yourself that you'll suffer foot-in-mouth disease and say something stupid. Or you may worry about your appearance so much that you don't bother to listen. If you're preoccupied with such distractions, you'll speak haltingly and appear frazzled and jittery. Replace these thoughts of self-sabotage with mental messages that reinforce your eagerness to listen and learn. Realize that the way you carry yourself matters far more than if your lipstick's fading or your tie is crooked.

> **⚠ CAUTION!**
> **I'm Losing It!**
> When networking, don't dwell on whether you're losing face or embarrassing yourself. If you're unhappy with your appearance or you let slip a remark that you instantly regret, plow onward. Banish doubts such as "I look terrible today" or "I sure sounded dumb saying that" or "I think I just insulted him by mistake." You'll bounce back more quickly from any bouts of embarrassment if you persevere and continue to breathe life into the conversation.

2. Fear of rejection. You're on a high now that you've been promoted into management. The last thing you want to do is jeopardize your heightened sense of worth by entering into conversations with people who might look down on you or seem to dismiss you. The result is you avoid placing yourself at risk of being rejected. There's a reason almost everyone fears rejection: it happens to almost everyone—and it hurts.

But consider the odds. If you launch 10 cold chats a week with both outsiders and colleagues within your organization, one (or maybe two in a really bad week) may lead to rejection. The other person might respond to your friendliness by withdrawing in a huff or making snide or condescending comments. But it's a numbers game. There's no reason to fear rejection if you keep plowing away and networking with more people. Some setbacks come with the territory, but they shouldn't stop you from making progress.

3. Fear of boredom. Your time is money. You have a full agenda. You find most people you meet intolerable bores. You conclude that stopping to chat in the hall or on your way to the taxi stand after a conference is a big waste. The chance that you'll get trapped with a loudmouth or a braggart is enough to keep you from saying hello. You've had your share of one-way encounters where you yearned to escape, and that's one of the reasons you hate to network. But the solution isn't to give in to your fear. Rather, try to awaken your curiosity and learn from even the most annoying or talkative people. Give them a chance to stir your interest. Don't say to yourself, "I'm bored and trapped" after just 30 seconds. Suspend your judgment until a few minutes pass and you give yourself a fair chance to extract some valuable piece of information from the speaker.

Mingling with Outsiders

Now that you're a manager, you will probably attend more training programs, conferences, and other networking events. This enables you to expand your list of contacts both inside and outside your industry. But it also means mingling with nosy outsiders who may take advantage of your openness to extract valuable information.

While you should forge relationships with people you like and respect, networking with outsiders can backfire if you reveal proprietary information or get too cozy with the competition. In your eagerness to gain acceptance, you may tell others about your company's growth plans and how you fit in. Or you may wind up giving negative opinions about a notorious bigwig in your industry—only to learn that the other person admires the individual you loathe.

In any networking situation, it's wise to ask great questions and get others to do most of the talking. That's even more important when you're meeting outsiders. You can't say something you regret later if you keep quiet for most of the conversation.

Another danger of networking with people outside your organization is that they'll try to "top"

> **Here's My Answer**
> TRICKS OF THE TRADE
>
> Don't feel obliged to answer every question you're asked. You can make friends without blindly supplying whatever information others request. If a competitor wants to know your unit's gross sales or the status of some litigation involving your firm, don't blurt out an answer. Instead, ask a question in return, such as "Why are you curious about that?" Remain pleasant but vigilant. Volley back questions and you'll keep a conversation lively—without getting yourself in trouble.

you. They may want to reinforce their own self-importance by showing off how much more power or influence they exert at their company or how much more experience or expertise they possess.

Don't take offense too quickly if someone contradicts you or tries to upstage you. Successful networkers give strangers the benefit of the doubt—at least once. Rise above your initial judgments so that you can get to know someone better. If after 10 minutes it's clear you're dealing with a nonstop braggart, then call it quits.

In many cases, however, you can forge bonds with others by bypassing their faults and letting them show their good side. Just keep them talking and resist sweeping indictments of their character. Above all, don't rush to disagree with what you hear or you'll put people on the defensive. Stay neutral in the first few minutes to make your networking pay off.

Also beware of turning your networking chats into gripe sessions. Never complain too much about your job to a stranger. The person sitting next to you at a seminar may know your boss and relay everything you said. Tell an outsider only what you would say to an insider at your organization. Or imagine that everything you say is being piped into your boss's office. That should remind you to use discretion.

Finally, never network out of desperation. Too much neediness is a turnoff. Say you've decided you want a new job. You meet a hiring executive at a firm where you'd love to work. Rather than engage in genial, interesting conversation by asking

---

Smart Managing

Cite Your Source, Please

Nothing kills a networking encounter as much as contradiction. If you think you hear a misstatement or an inaccurate fact, don't say, "That's wrong" and offer an instant correction. Instead, challenge others with a question, such as "How did you arrive at that?" Or in a curious, friendly tone, cite a source that clashes with what they said, "That's funny. *The Wall Street Journal* reported something different last week."

smart, stimulating questions, you come on strong and almost beg for help. The more you push, the more the executive pulls away.

Greet outsiders with enthusiasm, but don't overdo it. If you want something from them, keep it to yourself during the first few minutes as you get to know each other. Let your request arise naturally from the conversation. Ideally, you want them to ask you if there's anything they can do to assist you. And the best way to make that happen is to shower them with attention, keep them talking, and drop short, subtle hints.

Rainmaking in Action

When Jim became a manager, his boss told him that he was now expected to bring more business to the firm. So Jim refined his networking skills in an effort to become a "rainmaker"—a key contact who could attract wealthy clients. Jim attended industry conferences and approached attendees by asking, "What brings you here?" Most of them would volunteer their needs, such as seeking ways to manage change better or comply with ever-changing employment laws. Jim would ask more questions, but before each follow-up question he inserted one statement, such as "My other clients say the same thing" or "That's funny, because my firm solves those kind of problems for our clients." Soon, the people he met grew so curious that they started asking Jim about his firm's services.

Manager's Checklist for Chapter 12

❑ Network with a positive attitude and radiate professionalism. Maintain a pleasant facial expression, make eye contact, and stand up straight.

❑ Introduce yourself without fanfare. Just extend your hand and say, "Hi, I'm ...." You don't need a fancy opening line.

❑ Ask lots of questions. Look for opportunities to express genuine enthusiasm at the answers.

❑ Keep a log of your networking activity. Note any key details you hear and any commitments either party makes.

❏ Raise your visibility in your organization by networking aggressively. Offer to join cross-departmental teams, speak to other units, and ask advice.

❏ Fight off fears of networking by confronting them head-on. Acknowledge your anxieties and examine why they inhibit you.

❏ Watch what you say when meeting outsiders. Don't reveal too much about your employer. Ask more questions than you answer.

Index